Maximum Sunlight

Meagan Day

WITH PHOTOGRAPHS BY

Hannah Klein

*Avery,
we adore you!*

Mear M.

Hanh K

(it's true)

WOLFMAN BOOKS

However the city may really be, beneath this thick coating of signs, whatever it may contain or conceal, you leave Tamara without having discovered it. Outside, the land stretches, empty, to the horizon; the sky opens, with speeding clouds.

– Italo Calvino, *Invisible Cities*

Sky, sand, sky, sand, sky, sand

Most of unincorporated America is relatively civilized. Beyond the borders of small towns we encounter rural houses, roads, crop fields, livestock, scattered machinery, an array of anthropogenic junk. In the East there is scarcely an unobstructed acre, but even in the West we eventually spot power lines, drilling equipment, ranch fences.

But the edges of Tonopah, Nevada are sharp. There are houses and trailers with yards full of trampolines and car parts, and then suddenly there is only earth and sky. Tonopah, Nevada is an island of civilization in a vast humanless sea.

In the desert, up is sometimes difficult to distinguish from down. After heavy rains, water pools between the blackbrush and mirrors the stratosphere. Just after sunset the crisp horizon dissolves into a hazy bluish band. An inverted Fata Morgana will sometimes appear, actual hills collapsing into an imaginary limit. Tough bald hills slope at impossible angles, as if molded under the heel of a giant. It's easy to envision dinosaurs pounding this dry terrain with legs the size of refrigerators.

In Tonopah, I meet a man who warns me of the dangers of driving off-road in the desert at dawn and dusk. He crashed doing this once, going 120 mph on his three-wheeler. "I broke my neck out in the dunes and ripped my face off," he says. "I told them there was no way I was going to the hospital, to just give me a beer and wipe the sand out of my lips and my eyes."

This man has just spent a night in jail for a DUI and is sipping plain Coke through a straw. "I know where it sits now, the three-wheeler," he says, "and every time I see it I just get flashbacks to when I was flying off it – sky, sand, sky, sand, sky, sand. And that's why you don't ride at twilight. At twilight, you can't tell what a shadow entails."

The Cascadian Race

In the centuries since the arrival of Europeans, Nevada's Great Basin has inspired scores of esoteric origin theories. In 1924, "Was the Garden of Eden Located in Nevada?" made the front page of the *San Francisco Examiner*. The article was about the research of archaeologist Alain Le Baron, who claimed to have found petroglyphs not far from Tonopah that resembled Egyptian and Chinese characters, but predated both. He called the petroglyph site the Hill of a Thousand Tombs and believed it was evidence of an alternative anthropological timeline. His theory held that a prehistoric society called the Cascadian Race originated in Nevada and proceeded from there to populate the rest of the world.

Earlier yet, in 1917, an amateur geologist named Albert E. Knapp claimed to have found a fossilized human footprint from the Triassic period – the imprint of a shoe made of stitched dinosaur hide. This led him to believe that humans and dinosaurs had coexisted in Nevada's Great Basin 200 million years ago.

The *New York Times* took Knapp's finding somewhat seriously, as did Nobel Prize-winning Oxford scientist Frederick Soddy, who used it to support his pet theory of a superior race of prehistoric humans that destroyed itself after achieving scientific mastery over atomic energy. In Soddy's account, the sophisticated civilization made a technical mistake that wiped them out, leaving us – their more primitive counterparts – behind to literally reinvent the wheel.

These theories share a design: desertion by superior progenitors, the Great Basin as the point of origin for a flourishing society that eventually evacuates the region. This motif of abandonment can be located, too, in less fringe mythologies of the Nevada desert. Nevada, like California, experienced a Gold Rush that produced enormous wealth in the late 19th and early 20th centuries. Tonopah was known as a place where millionaires were minted. But the money made in Nevada boomtowns was soon taken elsewhere, mainly to California or back East in the pockets of savvy capitalists. Briefly, many of these towns were opulent. Now they are the residue of imperial advancement. Decade by decade their elegance fades.

"What do you think people in big American cities think about Tonopah?" I ask a woman in her fifties named Linda who's smoking a Winston 100 inside a casino called the Tonopah Station. "Like on the East and West Coast," I explain, "places like L.A. and New York."

She's playing electronic keno, a game that has a reputation as a working-class diversion – it was once considered too blue-collar, even, for gambling houses on the Las Vegas Strip. All around us colorful lights flash on gaming screens. The décor in the Tonopah Station is Western-fantasy, all wagon wheels and old saloon signage. The soundtrack is contemporary country, punctuated by bleeps from the gaming machines. The bar adjacent to the gaming room is doing decent business though it's only one in the afternoon.

"Well, aside from Vegas, I don't think they think about us at all," she says matter-of-factly, ashing into a tray provided by the house. "They probably don't know what Tonopah is, though it used to be a big important town. But we're out here."

Counter-eaters

The first time I passed through Tonopah, I lost an hour wandering its complicated streets, wide-eyed and straining with curiosity. I took one photograph on that first encounter. It shows the window of a white brick house. On the window-sill is a gold trophy. I remember that it was snowing. The trophy pricked me, a small sharp surprise, like what Roland Barthes means when he writes about the *punctum*, that subtle aspect that demands acute attention and inspires a ground-swell of emotional attachment for reasons that elude reason. Tonopah itself is unsentimental. Its relics are not enshrined so much as worked around, even ignored. But I grew nostalgic all the same. I lost the photograph, but I see it clearly in my mind.

That first visit, I was especially transfixed by the Clown Motel, a pair of shabby two-story blue buildings at the edge of town. A plywood cutout in the shape of a clown points to a hand-painted sign announcing that truckers are welcome. Directly adjacent to the motel is a Gold Rush-era graveyard, a few paces from the parking lot. I stared at the motel in amazement thinking *Why does this exist? Who the hell lives here, works here?* I had no frame of reference.

The route between Reno and Vegas is five hundred miles of America with essentially zero cultural profile. That's roughly the distance between Boston and Washington D.C., a stretch that encompasses hundreds of hyper-distinct cultural enclaves. Even rural Nevadans themselves, like Linda at the casino, will admit that they are neither contradictions to nor embodiments of any particular social archetype. The nation draws a blank on rural Nevada.

In 1940, the Works Progress Administration published a guidebook to the state that betrays a kind of sour-grapes attitude toward Nevada's abandonment in the broader American imagination:

> Relatively few Americans are familiar with this land. If the citizen of other states is asked what he knows about Nevada, he is apt to laugh and mention gambling and divorce… Pressed for the state's physical characteristics, he will usually mention the Great Basin, envisioned as a huge hollow bowl… There are various reasons for this vast ignorance about the sixth largest state in the Union, but the chief one has always been the reticence of Nevadans themselves. They have always known their State's great beauty and are unusually sensitive to it, but humbled by long neglect on the part of the vast traveling public, it is only recently that they have begun to tell the world about Nevada.

And yet, when it comes time to enumerate the specificities of Nevadan culture, all the writers can muster is that Nevadans like to *eat at counters*, a characteristic so trivial and generic as to be absurd.

> It is doubtful whether there is a restaurant in the state without one; even the smartest places feature counters. Usually the board is high and the stools are mounted on a small platform. No Nevadan is quite sure why he likes 'counter-eating'.

Rural Texans have the stalwart cowboy, Iowans have the forthright yeoman, and Mainers have the hard-bitten seafarer with rubber boots up to his knees. Nevadans have the counter-eater. Evidently I am not the first to grasp at straws.

In recent years, perhaps Cliven Bundy's high-profile standoff with the federal government has replaced the counter-eater of yore with the modern right-wing libertarian weapons stockpiler. But that still doesn't explain what a clown-themed motel is doing next to a graveyard in the middle of the treeless wilderness, or what that trophy was doing in that window.

For years, I'd think of Tonopah and be socked with the realization no matter what dramas and excitements visited my own life, some kind of existence continued out there in the desert, inscrutable to me. My enigmatic compatriots – I was and remain both curious about and troubled by this blind spot. I came to Tonopah to write, eventually, not because I wanted to answer a specific question, but because I had no idea what kinds of questions even applied.

We are after freedom

From the balcony of a dive bar amid a cluster of short-term residences called Humbug Flats, you can see every building in Tonopah. Small ranch-style houses with tidy facades alternate with puzzling complexes of shacks, sheds and mobile homes. The town sits in a saddle slung between steep hills, and the houses are crowded together, gradually terraced on the gentler slopes.

Tonopah is a striking anomaly, a small town in the middle of a great desert characterized by relative density rather than by sprawl.

The cause of this peculiar urban geography is that Tonopah is completely surrounded by public land. You can't build on it, but you can do just about anything else – hunt and trap, rummage for rocks and artifacts, drive your four-wheeler or pre-runner as fast as your heart desires. At the town's border, roads turn to dirt and extend faintly across the desert toward distant purplish mountains.

I'm told that there are two forms of entertainment in

Tonopah: drinking and off-roading. People drink because of the isolation – "there's nothing else to do" – while the off-roading is a consequence of proximity to hundreds of miles of unobstructed public land. So these recreational proclivities spring from the same source: the desert, which functions as both the town's playground and its quarantine.

Tonopah sits roughly halfway between Vegas and Reno on route US-95, about three and a half hours away from each. Its population is less than 3,000, and even at that it's the biggest town for more than a hundred miles in any direction. To the west is the imposing Sierra Nevada mountain range, with its snowy crests and flamboyant vistas. On the coastal side of the Sierras is California's productive Central Valley and its lush coastline. On the inland side of the divide spans the Great Basin, an arid region characterized by spindly mountain ranges stretching north to south and the flat desert valleys between them. From an airplane, the ranges look like slithering snakes.

Wallace Stegner wrote that one has to get over the color green in order to appreciate the American West. Natural green is a rare sight in the region around Tonopah, but hypnotic combinations of bruised purple and burnished gold at sunrise and sunset make a decent substitute.

In the bar of the Mizpah Hotel – built in 1907, carefully restored in 2011 after long abandonment, and now the most upscale business in town – I overhear two men introducing themselves to the bartender as federal employees. "The dreaded BLM," they say, and laugh. The Bureau of Land Management controls nearly 48 million acres in Nevada, about 67 percent of the state. Its mission is sprawling and contradictory – it monitors the health of plants and wildlife, maintains trails and recreational areas, and issues permits for drilling, mining, and cattle grazing.

With so many interests competing for its use, Nevada's BLM land is a battleground for opposing visions of the role of the federal government and the meaning of the term "public." Consider the Cliven Bundy standoff: Bundy was up against the agency over unpaid cattle-grazing fees, a private disagreement that quickly turned ideologically epic. "We are after freedom," he told the press of his ad-hoc encampment of far-right armed militiamen. "We are after liberty. That's what we want." The BLM was the enemy in the Bundy party's fight for nothing less than independence.

In theory, the people of Tonopah are not thrilled about the BLM. They wrinkle their noses at its mention – to many it's both a symptom and agent of federal authoritarianism, bureaucratic tyranny, and government overreach. At the same time, somewhat confoundingly, people tell me that Tonopah is a stronghold of individual liberty (one calls it "the last bastion of free America") precisely because they can largely do whatever they want out in the desert. The very same people who despise the BLM call the neighboring desert "the people's land" and refer to it proudly as "my backyard." There would be no bobcat trapping or informal desert drag racing if the land were private.

Managed though it is, BLM land is the freest and most open land in America. Perhaps the people of Tonopah have grown accustomed to a degree of autonomy with which the rest of us are unfamiliar, for their primary complaint about BLM land is that it's not free enough.

Horse management

I stop in at the University of Nevada in Reno and speak to Leonard Weinberg, an expert on grassroots right-wing politics, about the political landscape of Nevada. Nevada owes its blue-state badge largely to the Reno and Las Vegas metro areas, he tells me. The rural parts, by contrast, are characterized by staunch libertarianism.

"Nevada has the lowest rate of church attendance of any state in the union," Leonard says. "So it's not like the South. What we call the Cow Counties, including Nye County where Tonopah is, are overwhelmingly right-wing Republican, but the issues that excite people there aren't questions of morality and traditional values like you have with Southern religious right-wingers. Additionally, racial prejudice is not the driving force of right-wing politics here the way it is in the South."

Instead of the Ku Klux Klan or Christian family values groups, far-right organizations and movements here primarily include the Tea Party, the Sovereign Citizens, the

Oath Keepers, and various armed militias united in their deification of the founding fathers, fear of socialism, hatred of the federal government, contempt for taxation, mistrust of all politicians, and abiding commitment to the Second Amendment. "The main issue that gets people going is the government telling them what to do with their property," Leonard tells me.

"What's the situation with the wild horses?" I ask. I've read that they're a major source of tension between the federal government and rural Nevadans.

"Wild horses are accused of eating too much rangeland, harming cattle operations," he says. "There's a tussle that goes on between ranchers' associations and the environmental types who are defenders of wild horses. The ranchers want fewer wild horses roaming this territory."

They got their wish in 2007, when seventy-one wild horses wandered onto the Tonopah Test Range, a highly classified military base, and died of nitrate poisoning after drinking the water there. This was not the first year horse poisoning had been recorded there – Tonopah Test Range employees were even known to have operated a betting pool to guess how many would die. The poisoning may not have been intentional, but neither was it unwelcome.

At the Mizpah Hotel bar, one of the BLM employees – an abandoned mine specialist – explains, "They're not really wild. They're feral, and they need to be managed somehow. So there's a federal program to manage them, and there are areas called horse management areas, or HMAs." The bureau, for its part, is "just trying to deal with the situation and listen to all sides the best we can."

I ask Leonard if rural right-wingers in Nevada are

patriotic. "They would probably tell you that they are," he says, "but that's debatable. I remember there was one Iraq War general who retired to Douglas County," a bit west of Tonopah, "and said that it reminds him of Iraq – everyone hates the American government and they all have weapons. There are people here for whom the Second Amendment is the only part of the Constitution with which they're familiar, and they consider defending it to be the ultimate act of patriotism."

"Is immigration a big right-wing issue in Nevada?" I ask.

"Sure, there's anti-immigrant sentiment in Nevada. But even that manifests more as loathing for the federal government than for individual Hispanic people. There's racism here, no doubt," he concedes, but there's also an individualist live-and-let-live streak that precludes certain forms or manifestations of prejudice that one finds in other conservative regions, namely the South.

"Keep in mind that the Nevada state nickname is Battleborn," he says, "because it was created during the Civil War as a non-slave-owning state. There's a fair amount of pride associated with that here. In a sense, the anti-slavery cause relates to the local theme of 'Leave me alone, do whatever you want to do but just stay out of my way.'" He laughs and says, "In fact, now that I think about it, that seems like it should be the state motto," in place of the ill-fitting All for Our Country.

Time machine

Tonopah is, in many ways, the apotheosis of rural right-wing Nevada. It's an isolated town in an isolated and isolationist state, a self-reliant town in a state where rural residents not only prize but insist on self-reliance, a town fully surrounded by federal land in a state that feels besieged by the federal government.

Unsurprisingly, many people I speak to in Tonopah are vocal about their right-wing political views. I hear that the government is planning to confiscate private citizens' firearms, that Barack Obama is not an American citizen, and that Obamacare is the biggest current threat to American liberty besides Islamic terrorism.

Most people I speak to, however, tell me they don't care for politics at all. I ask one woman whether she's more liberal or conservative. "I don't follow that stuff," she answers, annoyed. "All I know is I wish I had a time machine so I could go back to the 1700s with George Washington, back in the time when people didn't rob their neighbors so much."

Another person tells me, "I don't talk about politics. I can't do anything about it anyway, and that pisses me off. And I don't vote because they already know who's gonna win."

At one point I ask a room full of people, who've all been open and obliging so far, if I can talk to them about their political views. They bellow "No!" in unison, followed by rowdy laughter and clinking of beer bottles. One quietly mumbles that he likes Hillary Clinton, and his friend quickly interjects, "He doesn't speak for us," but declines to clarify her own political leanings.

Perhaps the people I'm speaking to consider political inquiry an invasion of privacy. Or maybe they really don't care – maybe Tonopah is simply too far removed, geographically and in its unique local concerns, from the nation at large for people to feel invested in national politics. It's possible that, just as America has neglected rural Nevada in elaborating its pantheon of cultural archetypes, so too have the people of rural Nevada turned a blind eye to the goings-on of the nation.

Maximum sunlight

Like an island, Tonopah is strictly circumscribed. There are limitations on its latitude—because of the BLM, the town its prohibited from sprawling. The population remains steady and financial resources scarce, so Tonopah residents don't build up, either. They just don't build much at all.

Many live in timeworn houses or inventive structures made from repurposed parts of other edifices. Architecturally, the town speaks a junkyard vernacular. Every sliver of space is a profusion of materials and textures — corrugated tin, rusted steel, weathered wood, chipped paint, mortar, rebar, drywall, old cars and furniture put out to pasture. Whatever your vantage point, you can see a whole lot without turning your head.

Beyond the town limits, the nearest trees can be found in neighboring Goldfield. The natural landscape is characterized by stony crags and desolate flats meagerly populated with nondescript grasses and shrubs. Ninety percent of the earth's surface is pale dirt so dry that it whips into dust at the slightest disturbance.

If you say the word "plant" to people in Tonopah, their minds first turn to the Crescent Dunes Solar Energy Project just west of town.

The solar plant is a mystical arrangement – 10,000 mirrors surround a 600-foot tower filled with molten salt. From the highway, in the afternoon when the sunset illuminates the tip of the tower, Crescent Dunes looks like a candle flickering in the desert. From overhead, with its mirrors arranged in a circle nearly two miles in diameter, it looks like a throng of pilgrims encircling the Grand Mosque of Mecca. All day long the mirrors swivel to capture maximum sunlight.

The rollout of Crescent Dunes has been mostly quiet and efficient. Only one occurrence betrayed the formidable, almost occult power of the machinery. For unspecified reasons, employees staging a test adjusted the mirrors so that they directed light at a focal point 1,200 feet above ground, twice as high as the tower. The suspended field of light attracted birds, which flew into the solar flux and were immediately incinerated. Scientists noted over a hundred "streamers" – trails of smoke and vapor – left behind by individual cremated birds.

The plant's owners apologized for the "avian incidents" and redirected the mirrors back down at the tower. Since then, the plant has continued preparatory testing without drama, but locals regard it with more trepidation than they did before. Some say it's badly built. They say if you look at it closely, you can see that it leans.

Between 2011 and 2013, over 4,000 people worked on the construction of Crescent Dunes. Many were Tonopah residents – particularly those hired to assemble the mirror panels – but the majority were specialists from elsewhere who left once construction was completed. A company called Cobra brought out a lot of Spaniards. There were hundreds of them during the preliminary stages, living in the Mizpah Hotel or Humbug Flats or even the Clown Motel. There are still a handful of Spaniards in town. They speak poor English, but drink and play pool with the locals.

Now only a few dozen people are employed to oversee daily operations on the site. Crescent Dunes mines sunlight, and like every mine in the history of the region, its peak employment window was astonishingly brief. This is the nature of industry here: residents wait for news of a new mine or plant or infrastructure project, strike while the iron's hot, and know not to expect anything permanent.

Thunderhead

I'm standing on Main Street looking for people to interview, feeling graceless and unprepared. Finally I get up the nerve to approach an older man in Carhartt overalls, a bucket hat, and dark sunglasses. He's sitting on a bench with an ancient laptop balanced on his knees. "Hi," I say too eagerly, surprising him. I scale it back. "I'm writing about the town. Can I talk to you about living here?"

He takes off his sunglasses and sizes me up. "Well, I'm not from here originally," he answers, then pauses, searching for the most concise way to let me down.

"Ma'am," he finally decides, "I'm a Baptist minister, and my opinion of Tonopah is not high. There are behaviors in this town to which I'm not accustomed." He smiles, pleased with his pithy assessment. "So I'd better pass."

The first person to accept my invitation is the town bookseller. He leads me through his store, its shelves abundant with volumes crammed in at strange angles, to a dim kitchen lined with dark green floral wallpaper. We sit in folding chairs with our elbows propped on a red-and-white checkered plastic tablecloth. "So," he begins, but says nothing else, evidently waiting for me to speak first.

I ask his name. Joe. I ask his age. Seventy-three. I ask if he's from here. He shakes his head. "So what brought you to Tonopah?"

"Well first," he says, "what brings you here? You writing a travel piece?"

"Sort of," I say, "but I'm less interested in tourism and more interested in daily life. I used to drive through here sometimes and it always gave me a strange feeling. It's like its own planet, so far away from everything else. And I did some research and learned about the mines, and the wild horses, and the nuclear testing, and the military planes and everything." My face flushes. "So I'm just curious, I guess."

This is good enough for Joe. He leans back and folds his arms across his chest. "I was living out in California before this," he begins. "I moved here in 2008, after I retired. I'm a sober alcoholic, been sober for over 24 years. My sponsor in AA was dying, and I hadn't quite figured out what I wanted to do yet in my retirement. He said he wanted me to take Alcoholics Anonymous to the wilderness."

Having already decided on Nevada, Joe conducted an internet search for the town that had the most drug and alcohol arrests and the paltriest recovery resources. "Winnemucca and Tonopah tied as far as the most arrests, but Winnemucca already had meetings," he says.

Joe lives off his pension and savings, and opened the store for essentially the sole purpose of establishing a space for Alcoholics and Narcotics Anonymous meetings. In the back of the store is a meeting room with inspirational posters on the wall, pamphlets for the taking, and folding chairs assembled around a white folding table. The shop barely makes any money, he admits. And he's not particularly bookish himself – he tells me he's read only two books since he opened the place seven years ago. The first was a mystery novel, and the second was "more scientific," though he can't remember the subject matter.

I ask him what the impact of the meetings has been so far. "It's given some people their life back," he says. "It's given some people life who never even had a life. I started drinking at ten years old," he confides easily. Like many sober alcoholics, he has his story down pat, each phase measured in years and each turning point attached to a precise age, a highlight reel from a life of internal struggle. "There's a lady in town who started drinking at nine years old. She comes to the meetings. Until you learn to live a different way, you don't know any better."

"We just had a man named Chuck die at the end of June," he continues. "He was six years sober. He used to be a fall-down drunk and he used drugs intravenously. He had just lost his job shortly before he came to AA, and was several months behind on his rent. He was ready to commit suicide." Chuck heard about the meetings at Joe's bookstore through a friend, and Joe helped him get back on his feet, putting him to work shelving books.

"Chuck died right here in this store of a heart attack," Joe tells me, nodding toward the entrance where a sagging couch greets visitors, be they customers or addicts. On the coffee table in front of the couch is a jigsaw puzzle, only the perimeter completed. Joe's balding Chihuahua shivers in its tiny dog bed. The carpet is brown and flecked with lint. The shelves in the back are draped in clear tarps for a repair job that's been put on indefinite hold.

Despite Chuck's early death, his body battered by decades of substance abuse, Joe considers his story a success. He shows me a framed picture of a man grinning through a biker beard that's as grey and dense as a thunderhead. "Chuck was a good friend," he says with soft eyes.

I ask him why people drink so much here. "That's what there is to do," he replies.

"How many bars are there in town?"

"There's the Mizpah, the Tonopah Liquor Company," he counts on his fingers, "the Station House, the Bug Bar, the Bank Club, the Tonopah Brewery. And there used to be the Club House. That was a hard-drinking dive bar. A miserable place. Bar fights every night. Closed earlier this year, but the drunks still sit right out front on the sidewalk there."

Then he says, with sudden urgency, "I got out before I killed anyone. I had blackouts all the time. I could've killed someone in a bar fight or car accident and not even known why I was in jail when I came to. I said I couldn't do that."

He shakes his head vigorously. "And people in this town, they're suffering. So you see? That's why I'm here."

Sensitives

"The people are still living on the history," says Wilma, who works in the office of the Clown Motel. "Many of them are descendants of the original miners. And many are miners themselves. Out in Round Mountain or Silver Peak, mostly. There are generations of them who've lived here since the 1900s, and their attitude is pretty much still the same. Wild West."

"What do you mean by that?" I ask her. She's probably in her early fifties but has girlish face and round, earnest eyes. Her waist-length red hair is bound by a scrunchy at the nape of her neck. When she speaks, each *r* sound shades slightly into a *w*.

"The miners used to drink a lot," Wilma replies. "That was their only other thing besides mining. They would sleep in the mines for like seven days, and they would come out and they didn't have family to go to because they were single guys or their family was way back somewhere else, so the only thing they had was the alcohol. That's staying, that kind of attitude."

I tell her that she's not the first person to bring up booze when explaining the town to me, and her laugh betrays a bit of concern. "Alcohol use in this town is tremendous," she says. "I mean, wow. It's a huge situation." Her affect is now serious, a bit stunned. "I don't know much about the drugs. Meth is pretty prevalent here, I know that. But the alcohol, yikes, it's way out there. You can see it at night in the town. It keeps 'em low, keeps 'em icky."

Wilma pauses to take a phone call, and my eyes scan the room. To my left are several shelves of clown figurines, over five hundred of them. A sign hanging in the middle reads:

SPECIAL CLOWNS FROM

AROUND THE WORLD NOT FOR SALE

Behind me are two life-sized clown dummies. One is an early iteration of Ronald McDonald, while the other is more of a Barnum & Bailey type.

"Don't look into that one's eyes," says Wilma, placing the phone back on the receiver. She gestures toward the old-timey one clad in a rainbow jumpsuit. Several fingers are missing from its life-size hands. Wilma was afraid of clowns when she first came to work here, she tells me. She's mostly gotten over it, but that one still strikes her as "a little off."

The Clown Motel sits at the western edge of town. For the phobic, there's no skirting the issue – there's a clown on every door and clown paintings above every bed. Adding to the potential fear factor is the cemetery right next to the motel, visible from nearly every vantage point.

"Are people freaked out by this place?" I ask. The smaller clown figurines are cheerful portrayals with over-sized shoes, accordions and juggling pins – vestiges of a time when clowns enjoyed more favor in the hearts of the masses. The whole history of clowns is on display: There are porcelain harlequins with cherubic faces and rosy cheeks, hobo clowns with patches on their pants and sympathetic frowns, and polka-dotted buffoons with frizzy orange hair poking out above their ears. One, however, is obviously a later creation, fabricated after John Wayne Gacy Jr. and the movie *It* transformed the clown into a popular object of dread. Teeth bared and eyes crazed, it's perched in a metal cage like a lethal zoo animal. This figurine is prominently displayed near the front desk, demonstrating a wry self-awareness on the part of the Clown Motel's management.

"Oh sure, people are scared," she answers. "But we still get a lot of business. Some people actually come here to face their fear. I've seen 'em faint and I've seen 'em scream. It's not uncommon to see somebody walk in and their face turn pure white." She tells me she's even met people who were sent here on the advice of their therapists.

"If you ask me, the Clown is not nearly as scary as the cemetery next door," she says. "There's a lot of paranormal activity there. We get tons of researchers. Psychic people, sensitives, ghost hunters. They always find something."

"What's a sensitive?" I ask.

"People that are so sensitive they can feel the entities around them," she explains. "Ghost hunters bring sensitives with them, and if the sensitives feel like something's going on, that's when they start their cameras. And sure enough, bam. There's a lot of activity in this town, because there was a lot of death here. The mines were so dangerous. A lot of death."

I ask her why she came to work in the Clown Motel if

she was afraid of clowns. "My husband and I were really down on our luck when we first arrived here," she answers. "We had a car that was acting like a real idiot." She explains that she was on her way from Texas to California when her car started to falter, just past Las Vegas. By the time they got to Tonopah, "the car decided that it didn't want to go any further," she laughs. "Piece of work is what it was."

She and her husband slept in their busted car in the parking lot of the Bank Club, a local small-time casino with an adjoining Chinese restaurant, for about three days. "Then one of the nice people at the grocery store told us, 'Hey, go talk to Hank P., he can help you out.' So we did and he offered us a job."

Hank P. owns the Clown Motel, along with a large share of the retail space on Main Street. I tell her I've already heard stories about Hank P., that he employs people who have no money, people who have substance abuse problems, homeless people, out-of-town drifters. I've heard that he gives them work at the Clown, or the pawnshop, or the Economy Inn, and that he often hooks these people up with places to stay. She nods her head in agreement with everything I'm saying. "He just cares," she says finally. "He cares about the people and the town. He's descended from one of the original families. He wants to rise the place up."

I don't tell her that in the few interviews I've conducted thus far I've also heard him called a loan shark and a slumlord, that I've heard him accused of exploiting the desperation of the local down-and-out. People seem either bitterly resentful of Hank P. or eternally grateful to him.

"He helps you get on your feet," Wilma continues. "Like Jeff. He's one of the hard-ups. He has a real problem with alcohol, major. And he comes off of it and he's a sane person, and then he leaves for a while. He does it in waves. It's a cycle. And Hank always hires him back."

I ask her if Hank ever has problems with the people he helps out. "Yeah, I mean sometimes he has to forcibly get the money from them because folks like to use and abuse. And he's a *strong* person." She emphasizes this by leaning forward across the counter. "You don't mess with Hank P."

"Is this a violent place?" I ask. Night is falling and my car is parked closer to the center of town, so I'll need to walk.

"Well there are bar fights," she says laughing, "so try not to get into one of those. We used to have a place called the Club House. That was a hang spot, but it just got closed down. It was a fighting, brawling kind of place. It was a really cool place though, with a beautiful old bar and a lot of history. People would go just to hang and let loose. It was *the* spot."

I tell her I'll avoid bar fights and thank her for her time. "Hey if you go to the cemetery," she adds, "just watch your phone battery. The cemetery always drains phone batteries."

Tiny

Outside the pawnshop is a sign that reads, "Free Lifetime Parking reserved for Hank P." He owns this building, and I've heard that Jeff works here. But even though it's the middle of the day, The Hock Shop is locked up and there's no one in sight. On the door is a hand-scrawled sign announcing three open beds in a mobile home, available immediately for solar or construction workers. The sign says to call Hank P. if interested, and that rooms at the Clown Motel are also available weekly or daily.

I keep walking down the block, past the Tonopah Liquor Company and the shuttered Club House. A middle-aged man sits on the sidewalk with an open beer in hand. I pass within two feet of him, but he doesn't lift his head.

On the other side of the Club House is a small storefront whose handwritten sign says The Hock Shop 2. A guy out front is holding a pair of dancing Native American dolls. He looks to be in his early forties, with unkempt blonde facial hair, sunburnt skin, and a jumble of improvised tattoos. I tell him I'm a writer working on a story about the town and ask him if he'd be up for an interview.

"Just as soon as I put price tags on these drunk Indians," he says with a chuckle. "They're for storing whiskey, see?" He shows me the openings where the liquor flows in and out.

I wince and say, "Oh. Look at that."

The shop is more like a storage unit, barely any attempt at organization or attractive display. The guy, named Zachary, invites me to sit in a metal folding chair, pushing aside an ashtray on a cluttered table so I can rest my arm. I take stock of his appearance: blue eyes, baseball cap, missing teeth.

Suddenly he remembers something and gets up. "Sorry," he says, turning the sign on the door from closed to open. "We're having a little sale. A lady in town, Barbie, her husband committed suicide two weeks ago, so I'm donating twenty percent of all my profits for the weekend to help her cover the funeral costs."

"Is Barbie a friend of yours?" I ask.

"Kind of. She works at Giggle Springs," he says, referring to the gas station and convenience store across the street. I later learn that the name is a mistranslation of the town's Paiute name, which does not mean "laughing water" as the original owner had believed. "She's a real nice lady that helps anybody out in town. When I came to this town I didn't have nothing. And the gentleman than owns this building gave me this store to run, gave me the house I live in, and everything else. So somebody helped me, and now it's my chance to help someone else." The gentleman, of course, is Hank P.

I ask him where he came from, and he says Arkansas,

though he's originally from Aberdeen, Washington. "The hometown of Kurt Cobain," he adds.

"How does Tonopah stack up?" I ask.

"It's a quiet little town," he says, "but there's too many alcoholics here. There are about twenty of them that sit out front of my store every day. It's irritating. A few of them live in apartments up above the Hock Shop. If you went into the Hock Shop and talk to that guy, his name is Jeff, he's drunk from the time he wakes up to the time he passes out."

"Jeff seems to have a real reputation," I say.

"Oh yeah," he confirms. "He comes into my store all the time and helps himself to my stuff. All my jewelry from Africa ended up in his store for sale."

"Do you live in these apartments back here?" I ask. He scoffs and says you couldn't pay him to live there. The apartments are on the backside of the building. I can see them from my motel room, and have observed the comings and goings of various men clad in dirty jeans, often accompanied by muscular off-leash dogs.

"Are the guys who live back there Hank P.'s guys?" Zachary nods his head yes. I ask if he's friends with any of them.

"No. I'm not friends with any of Hank P.'s guys," he says with a sneer. Zachary is himself one of Hank P.'s guys, but evidently envisions himself a cut above the rest. "Actually I can't say that. There is one guy that works for him as a mechanic that I'm friends with personally. But he and I have a similar background, so we get along pretty well. The other guys are all just a bunch of worthless drunks."

"Do you think it's good that Hank helps them out?" I ask.

"Yes and no," he responds. "It's good that Hank gives

them something productive to do for the day, otherwise they just sit here and bother people. But it's bad that he gives them the money that he does, because he knows they're just gonna go out and drink. That's the only time they come in and work for him is when they need money for booze. And I have a problem with that."

Bells jingle and a Latino man walks in, wobbly on his feet.

"Hey Lee," says Zachary coolly.

"Has anybody come in here and tried to sell you a DeWalt drill?" Lee asks, leaning on a cane to steady himself.

"Nobody's tried to sell me anything stolen," answers Zachary. "They know better. Everything that comes into my shop goes to the sheriff's department for thirty days and then comes back."

"That DeWalt cost me $170," Lee says in protest. "That sucks. That was expensive."

"Well, I'll keep my eyes out. If someone brings it in I'll snatch it up and call the sheriff's office."

"I think he left town," Lee says, shaking his head.

"Who was it?" Zachary asks. "Nate?" Lee nods yes, anger glowing in his eyes. "Nate left," Zachary confirms. "He owed Hank a lot of money. He split, man."

Lee is quiet, disappointed. Abruptly he lifts his cane and brings it down hard. "I hate thieves," he declares.

"Trust me, so do I," says Zachary. "I've had many thieves in here try and steal stuff from me. They were willing to go to jail for fifteen dollars – hey, fine by me. They don't realize that I can put handcuffs on 'em myself and take 'em to jail." He turns to me and straightens his back as he boasts, "I work for the sheriff's department here and in Mineral County. I can arrest people." Somehow I doubt this is entirely true.

Lee is silent, stewing. After a long pause he says resignedly, "Well you have my number," and turns to leave. Before he exits he looks over his shoulder and says, "Hey, you want these?" He's waving a stack of envelopes.

Zachary asks what they are.

"My bills!" says Lee, and laughs from his belly, his spirits temporarily lifted. The bells jingle again, and he's gone.

Zachary turns to me. "He's one of the drunks I was telling you about. He had a dog called Tiny. It was a really big dog. He had that dog for twenty years. And somebody from California come and hit it with a car, and it had to be put down. Lee's been drunk ever since."

Stuff out there that isn't there

Throughout the Cold War, the United States Air Force ran a classified program to test the capabilities of its aircraft against foreign fighter planes. The USSR-based Mikoyan-Gurevich Design Bureau was building exceedingly agile aircraft and supplying them to the United States' Cold War enemies. By the late 1960s, as the Vietnam War came into full swing, American air-to-air combat losses due to these planes – known as MiGs – were growing worrisome.

In 1967, under a program called Have Doughnut, the U.S. acquired a Soviet MiG from Israel. The plane had been handed over by an Iraqi fighter pilot who chose to defect rather than drop napalm on Iraqi Kurdish civilians. It was flown to top-secret Area 51, between Tonopah and Las Vegas, to be poked and prodded by the United States Air Force.

Over the next decade more captured MiGs were flown in, and secret dogfights began to take place over the Nevada desert. To keep the program under wraps, airspace was fully restricted and the area was blotted out in red ink on aerial maps – furtive measures that contributed to Area 51's prominent place in conspiracy theories about UFOs and insidious government plots.

In 1979, these foreign technology evaluation tests were relocated to nearby the Tonopah Test Range, known as Area 52. The fighter pilots there, known as the Red Eagles, lived in a dormitory called Mancamp, which consisted of "a chow hall, an Olympic-size stainless steel pool, bowling alleys and a sports field that was lit up at night," according to an interview given by pilot John Manclark after the official declassification of the secret program.

Some pilots played the role of aggressors – they were tasked with flying Soviet planes and replicating enemy tactics so that trainees could troubleshoot effective responses. Several pilots died flying the unfamiliar aircraft, for which the United States had no manuals. "We didn't know what ninety percent of the switches did," said Manclark. "We had one switch that we just labeled BOMB EXPLODE."

At the same time, Lockheed was busy building the F-117 Nighthawk at the Tonopah range. It was America's first stealth aircraft, designed to avoid radar detection in enemy airspace. The engineering of the F-117 was a highly classified black project and the Tonopah Test Range a black site. Thousands of personnel worked on the project, and were flown to Tonopah on Mondays and back out to the Las Vegas area on Fridays. They were prohibited from telling their families where precisely they went all week.

The United States government came up with a cover story involving a surrogate aircraft, justifying the program's existence to the civilian world and deflecting suspicion.

Early biometric technology was used to screen everyone who entered the base, and vehicles that came too close to the range were searched and their occupants warned away.

The F-117 flew only in the dark, and its manuals were kept inside a hyper-secure vault. The pilots were called Bandits and wore patches featuring scorpions, sphinxes, atomic symbols, grim reapers, and eagles with lightning emanating from their talons. One patch featured an image of the plane and the embroidered words, "To those who hide at night, beware of those in the shadows."

Eventually, the Nighthawk was ready for war. In 1991, leaflets rained down on Iraqi villages showing the plane wreaking havoc and warning civilians to "Escape now and save yourselves." The aircraft dropped thousands of bombs during the Gulf War, and continued to operate through the '90s.

Only one Nighthawk was ever lost to U.S. enemies – the aircraft, named Something Wicked, was shot down by Serbs in Yugoslavia in 1999. There is speculation that the missing equipment was acquired by China or Russia for study, bringing full circle Tonopah's relationship to the top-secret world of foreign aircraft exploitation.

While Tonopah's Area 52 is not as ubiquitous in conspiracy theories as neighboring Area 51, the site's combination of strict confidentiality and global impact lends itself to paranoid interpretations. Most residents know bits and pieces of what takes place in the desert outside their town, but nobody knows everything. Parts of the history are still classified, and secret projects are still underway.

Proximity to the genuinely clandestine inspires eccentric worldviews in locals, or at least an increased openness to what might elsewhere be considered crackpot conspiracy theory. But few people dwell near government black sites – information about the land we live on is readily obtainable, largely predictable, and often mundane. If secret plots are actually unfolding in your backyard, orchestrated by absentee elites intent on consolidating global power, it becomes difficult to dismiss other theories that follow the same pattern. For some residents of Tonopah, the mystery of nearby government activity is understandably destabilizing.

"Do a lot of people believe in UFOs around here?" I ask Wilma at the Clown Motel.

"Oh yeah," she says unreservedly, her eyes growing wide. "A lot of people have *seen* UFOs here. I'm one of them. I've seen multiple UFOs throughout my life. I know it sounds crazy. But I had people with me who witnessed it."

I ask her to describe what she's seen in Tonopah. "I've only seen one here," she says. "It was a couple years ago and I was walking home from work at the Clown. I saw this thing come flying in, no sound at all, right in the middle of town. There was no denying it was freaky. It did a little back and forth thing, a very intelligent type of movement, and then it went straight up into the universe. I mean, c'mon!"

"Why do you think people see so many UFOs here in this part of the country?" I ask.

"It could be the Indian reservations," she explains soberly. "That's a huge possibility. The governments are not allowed to touch the UFOs or even try to go after them in the reservation areas. I know that for sure. And the Native Americans are firm believers in UFOs. It's part of their whole thing."

Mounted on the wall to her left is a placard that boasts a silhouette of the F-117 against a map of the Middle East, pockmarked with little cartoon explosions. It reads "TONOPAH STEALTH – 1st to Strike In The Gulf."

I suspect that Wilma would believe in UFOs whether or not she lived near a secret government site. Throughout our conversation, she eagerly divulges theories about additional forms of paranormal activity (while she has not seen a ghost at the Clown, she has smelled one – it wafted in on a cold wind and "smelled like a very ancient perfume"). Other residents surprise me a bit more, like Clifford who works at Joe's bookshop.

A self-described computer nerd who moved here six years ago from Southern California, Clifford speaks matter-of-factly. "I help Joe out in the bookstore," he says, "but my skill set is more technical. Computer networks, information systems, business systems."

He gets excited when I mention the Tonopah Test Range and the stealth bomber built there. "Oh man, it's an awesome piece of war machinery," he says. "It's a killing machine. The designers were all told to design different parts – the wings, the cockpit. There was no collaboration whatsoever. That's how they keep the secrecy of the design." He relishes both the technical sophistication and the cloak-and-dagger gravity of the project.

"Somebody told me they're building another secret plane out there," I offer.

"That's what I heard," he affirms. "Man, the security measures that they have in place are serious. If you wander off the beaten path and end up on the test site, within minutes security will come out of nowhere and be all over you. It's very tightly controlled." I had read accounts of wayward explorers who suddenly found themselves surrounded by a swarm of military vehicles, unaware that they had trespassed from public into top-secret land.

I ask him if the secrecy has any effect on people living in town, if it fosters theories about covert activity. Clifford strikes me as a rationalist, and I'm expecting to chuckle together about local kooks. Instead he says, "I mean, I don't know. I've seen some pretty weird stuff myself that I have no explanation for here in Tonopah. I've seen flying objects that I couldn't identify. The flight path and the flight pattern, the maneuverability, there's nothing that we have that I'm aware of that can maneuver like that."

He continues, "I've seen glowing orbs in the sky. They go one direction and then another and then they just disappear. Then they reappear somewhere else, and it makes no sense."

I ask him if the flying objects could be military technology and not intelligent extraterrestrials. "Absolutely," he says, relieved by my suggestion. "Here in Nevada, there's so much open ground that it's a lot easier to test aircraft without having to worry about communities getting an eyeball on it. They mostly fly out in the middle of nowhere. Sometimes a camper or a hiker will see something, but they largely go undetected." He lights a cigarette and leans back in his chair, taking a long first drag. "The stuff we see is just one fraction of what goes on out there."

Later, I'm at the Tonopah Liquor Company conducting an interview when a man comes up to me and says quietly, "So you're a reporter."

I nod my head and he says, "I work for the government.

Listen. If you go up into the hills, find the golf balls. And when you've found the golf balls, look southeast. There's stuff out there that isn't there, if you know what I mean. It isn't there, but it is."

I never learn his name, and I never find the golf balls.

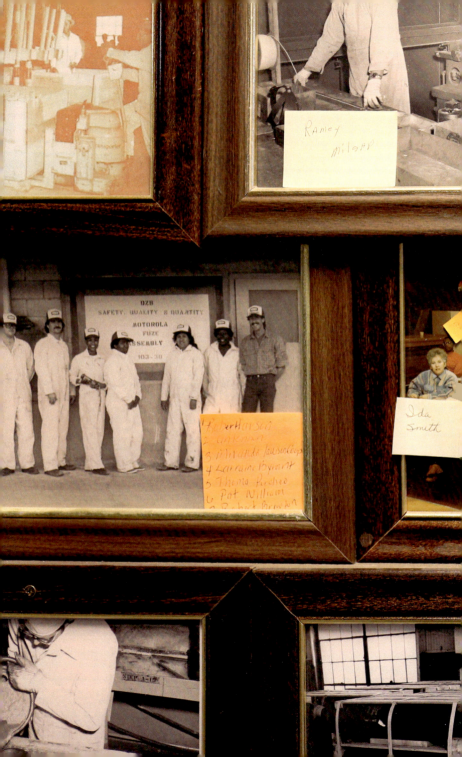

RAmey
MilsAP

DZB
SAFETY, QUALITY & QUANTITY
MOTOROLA
FUZE
ASSEMBLY
103-38

1 Robert Harris
2 Catherine
3 Miranda Gonzales
4 Lorraine Bryant
5 Thoma Perches
6 Pat Williams
7 Robert Brown

Ida
Smith

WHITE POWER

Back at the pawn shop, I ask Zachary how he feels about the Club House closing next door.

"I don't have an opinion on that or any bar in this town," he answers. "I don't go out drinking and doing all that stupid stuff. If I want a beer I go home and drink in my house, or I grab a six-pack, go out in the desert and ride my 4x4."

I ask him why he doesn't drink at the bars. "I like to fight too much," he says. "There's a lot of bar fights in this town."

"So it would be dangerous for you?"

"It wouldn't be dangerous for *me*," he answers, a bit offended. "I can fight. I can fight very well. Actually all my front teeth are gone from fighting. I used to make a lot of money to fight." He shows me his gums.

"How did you make money fighting?"

"Almost like the UFC," he explains, "but not sanctioned. In a back alley, in a parking lot, in a parking garage, wherever people were willing to show up for a fight and pay money and make bets." The kind of fighting he's describing is an echo: the boxer Jack Dempsey, who was briefly a bouncer at the Mizpah Hotel, is said to have engaged in unsanctioned fistfights for sport, literally across the street from where I'm talking to Zachary.

"I did that for a large portion of my youth," he continues, "and a little bit of my adult time. It hurts too much now. My hands are destroyed from fighting. So I just don't do it no more."

He holds out his hands, knotty from years of trauma. I see that he has knuckle tattoos, but they're so faded I can't interpret them.

"Have you had those tattoos removed?" I ask.

"Oh no, they're just old."

"What do they say?"

"White power," he answers without missing a beat. He spreads his fingers so I can see better.

My stomach lurches. "Are you a…" I scan my brain for the most appropriate terminology.

"A skinhead?" he offers, unfazed. "Not anymore. I walked away from Aryan Nations about fifteen years ago." He explains that he moved to Idaho when he was twelve to live on a twenty-acre compound near Hayden Lake and pretty much grew up there.

"It was the headquarters of the Aryan Nations until 2001," he tells me, and research bears this out. Richard Girnt Butler, the leader of the Aryan Nations and the Church of Jesus Christ–Christian, formed an encampment near Hayden Lake in the 1970s. It was shut down after the Southern Poverty Law Center sued the group, following an incident in which civilians were attacked.

I ask Zachary who took him to Hayden Lake as a twelve-year-old. "I can't talk about that," he says, eyes narrow.

"Okay," I say. "But wow, twelve years old is pretty young."

"It is, but I moved up quick. By the time I was fourteen I was a lieutenant at arms. We trained people to become skinheads. A lot of the rules that I set in motion then are still being followed today. Not allowed to do drugs, not allowed to drink alcohol. Nothing to defile your body at all."

I'm skeptical of the amount of power he claims to have wielded. I remember his boast about working in a civilian capacity for the sheriff's department, and suspect that he has an inflated sense of influence. Still, I don't doubt his affiliation with the Aryan Nations. Later I find records indicating that he lived in Idaho during the peak of skinhead activity, and all the dates he gives me in relation to Hayden Lake – the year it was established, the year he arrived, his age when he arrived, the year it shut down, his age when it shut down, and the total length of his stay – all line up. There are no discrepancies in that part of the story.

I ask him why he left the Aryan Nations. "I just grew up," he says. "There's too much stupid shit in this world to hate all the time. Life's too short. Hate kills you. So I just quit. Recently in Idaho I had a bunch of young kids walk up to me that were skinheads, and they said, 'Hey we know who you are.' I said, 'No, you don't know who I am.' 'Yes we do, we still follow your rules.' And I said again, 'No, you don't know who I am,' and I just walked off. And they looked at me like, *What the hell?* But I'm not a part of it anymore."

I ask him if he feels bad for those kids. "Yeah, because they're not being taught right," he says. "They're being taught to be gangbanger thugs. When I was a skinhead, it wasn't about being a racist. It was about getting my people what they had coming to them. It was more political. Now it's all about, oh look, there's a black kid, let's go kill him. I don't believe in that. You don't just go *kill* somebody because of their race. If there's a cause or a reason, then that's why you deal with it."

"So did they just let you walk away?" I ask. "I've heard that's basically impossible."

"I got permission. I had a good track record, good relations. And the camp at Hayden Lake closed, and everything was up in the air. So they let me leave. They still reach out to me though. They asked me to take care of these two skinheads who are hiding here in Tonopah, but I said I wouldn't do that. I'm not in that life anymore."

"Take care of them like hook them up, help them out?"

"No," he says, quietly amused. "Not that kind of taking care of."

"Oh," I say, realizing what he means.

"They're not hiding from the law," Zachary explains, "they're hiding from other skinheads. Because unlike me, they ran away."

He stops talking to light a cigarette. His grasp is shaky because of his distorted hands, and it takes him a few tries to get the lighter going.

"It's weird that I was a skinhead," he continues, blowing smoke, "because I'm a quarter Choctaw. I just found that out in the last year. As soon as I found out I got my buffalo skull put on." He pulls up his sleeve to show me a new tattoo, crisp lines and dark ink. Above and below the skull are the words CHOCTAW PRIDE.

"I've known all my life I was part Native American," he

says, "I just didn't know what, and I didn't know it was this much. So I just shut that part of my life out and claimed just the Scottish and Irish."

I ask him if he felt like he was keeping a secret about his heritage at Hayden Lake. "No," he says, "I just figured that I didn't have enough Native American blood to matter. I didn't know I had this much."

"Has finding out that you're part Native American changed your opinions on race?" I ask.

"I'm still a separatist," he answers, "and I always will be a separatist. I will not go outside of my race to produce children. Because it makes it harder on the child. I don't know how it is now, in this day and age." He waves his hand in the air, as though that information were immaterial to his point. Despite the revelation and the tattoo, a lifetime of exposure to racist dogma has left some indelible marks on his ideology, even in skinhead retirement.

He continues, "In Tonopah, for example, you're not welcome if you're another race. There are some Hispanics and a few blacks here, but they're just here to work. You don't see them out at night time partying and all that other stuff."

It's true that the groups of people I'd seen hanging together in bars at night were uniformly white, while I usually spotted non-white residents in workplace settings, like the town's one Mexican restaurant and one Chinese restaurant.

"So there's no open hatred?" I ask. "It's just socially segregated?"

"Yeah," he agrees. "There's nothing open in this town at all. It's pretty much behind everybody's backs."

He puts out his cigarette and we're quiet for a moment.

"Hey," he finally says, "do you want to see something?"

He points to a sign on the table that says DO NOT HUMP. "Do not hump," I read aloud, bewildered.

"No, under the sign," he clarifies, and I get out of my chair and lift it up to discover a stack of books. "That one on top is signed by Dwight D. Eisenhower." The book is a yellow clothbound volume with a signature scrawled on the front cover. I take a picture of the book, and check it against Eisenhower's signature when I get back to the motel room – not only does it look real, but there are other images of the same book autographed in the same unusual style, signature on the front. Still, it could be fake.

"I have another book, too. It's in Hank P.'s safe – I don't keep it in the store because it's worth too damn much. It's from 1847. *Jane Eyre.*" He pronounces the surname like "eerie."

"*Jane Eyre* by Charlotte Brontë?"

"Yeah, that's it," he says. "I paid ten cents for it. There's a kid who comes in here about once a week and sells me stuff from a storage unit that belonged to his grandpa."

"That must be worth thousands of dollars," I say, astonished. I remind myself to be skeptical, but I'm also excited by the possibility that an ex-skinhead pawnbroker in a small town in Nevada owns a first edition copy of *Jane Eyre*, for which he paid ten cents.

"Oh it's worth a ton," he agrees. I research online later and see that an 1847 copy brought in over 60,000 dollars at a recent auction.

"If you're sitting on a treasure chest," I ask him, "why are you still working here?"

"I get bored," he answers. "If I'm not doing this I'm out there riding my dirt bike. Riding hard for twelve hours in that desert is relaxing to me. That's my medication. That for me is what all these people who have nothing around here seek in the form of a pill or drugs or alcohol. At midnight it's the best. Turn off the headlights and drive, use the light of the moon to see where you're going, and just hope you don't hit a rock."

Their opinion, not mine

Dennis Avner is the most famous Tonopah resident in recent history, though not under his given name. Professionally he went by the name Stalking Cat, while his friends knew him as Cat Man. He holds the Guinness world record for most body modifications to look like an animal – in his case, a female tiger.

Avner was Native American, of Lakota and Wyandot heritage, born in Flint, Michigan. When he was a child, a medicine man allegedly bestowed Stalking Cat upon him as a totem, and he spent his life trying to embody his spirit animal in his physical appearance. He tattooed his face with the stripes of a tiger, got subdermal implants to change his face shape, flattened his nose, bifurcated his upper lip, made his earlobes pointy, had his teeth pulled to install feline fangs, wore labret piercings in his cheeks to which he attached whiskers, and on special occasions flaunted green contact lenses and a robotic tail.

His transformation made him famous in the body

modification and furry communities. He was a mainstay at conferences and appeared on multiple television shows, including *Ripley's Believe it or Not!*, *Larry King Live*, and shows on the BBC, VH1, and Animal Planet.

But despite his fame, Avner was by all accounts a lonely man. Throughout the '80s, '90s and early aughts he lived in San Diego working as a computer programmer. His friends were mostly people he met online and at conventions. He changed not only his appearance but also his behavior, eating raw meat and, according to people I met in Tonopah, licking himself clean instead of showering. "He didn't bathe like you and I," one person in Tonopah tells me. "You wouldn't want to be in the aisle next to him at the grocery store."

These practices made human intimacy hard to come by. "I liked the Cat Man," his agent Chuck Harris said in a 2015 interview. "He was a tortured soul, but he was a nice, sensitive human being. I really felt sorry for the guy because I know I was his best friend. And I am not the best friend for many people – especially someone I only see two or three times a year."

Through the California furry scene Avner met a couple who invited him to move with them Washington state. Unlike anonymously large San Diego, Whidbey Island was a tight-knit community, and he became a minor local celebrity. The paper regularly ran articles about him, one of which described him as a "cigarette-smoking, out-of-work, registered Republican who owns firearms and left California because he believes it's become a communist state."

In 2007, Avner ran into financial trouble and moved to

Tonopah, drawn there by a friend from the furry community, and perhaps also by his political beliefs – those who see California as a communist dystopia are apt to see Nevada as a libertarian paradise.

His reception in Tonopah was mixed. Most people insist that *they* had no problem with Avner, but others did. "Very intriguing, really warm individual," says Wilma at the Clown Motel. "He was very advanced in computers. But people were really judgmental of him because of what he did with his face."

"Were they openly mean?" I ask her.

"Sometimes," she answers. "They just didn't want him around. He was trying to get work and nobody would hire him, they thought he made a bad image for them."

Avner found occasional employment fixing computers around town, but his main source of income – aside from occasional cash flow related to appearances on TV or at conventions – was elderly and hospice care. "The elderly people loved him," Wilma tells me. "They were usually bored out of their skull, and he was interesting, not to mention good to them. He was kind to the people who were sick and dying."

Later, in a room full of daily hard drinkers who tell me they all know Cat Man, I ask if he used to drink with them. "No, he liked to smoke though," says one man.

"Smoke pot?" I ask.

There's laughter in the room, and the man responds, "I just said smoke, didn't say what." I learn later in the conversation that these people are meth users.

I ask the group if Avner had any money. "He had to," says one woman, "because he kept the power going, and the water. Not like he ever bathed."

In 2012, at age 54, Avner was found dead in his garage. The cause was a gunshot wound to the chest. The sheriff's department ruled his death a suicide, but there are plenty of people in town who suspect otherwise. One police officer tells me he can't discuss the case, but then says, "Look, Cat Man killed himself. There's no doubt about that. People in this town are just excitable."

Another person present for this exchange had been called out to clean up the scene, and agrees that it looked like a suicide. "He was upset about not being able to get his tail," he tells me.

"Tail?" I ask.

"From England," he says. "He wanted this special tail from England, and it looked like it wasn't going to happen."

Wilma tells me a different story. "The way the rifle was lying, the way *he* was lying. There was just no possible way somebody committed suicide that way." I ask her how she knows these details about the scene, and she explains that she had contact with Avner's brother. "He came into town ranting and raving, and he convinced me. There were just too many discrepancies."

"Was there any change in Cat Man's behavior or mood prior to his death?" I ask.

"Not that I saw," she answers. "He was really looking forward to doing stuff. He was gonna head overseas and do a tour before that happened. He didn't have the suicide tendency. I just didn't get that from him."

"If he didn't kill himself, who did?"

"There were some strange individuals. This place is different. You have a lot of eccentric people. This one person who was hanging with him for a bit there was really off. He was schizophrenic and all that, and Cat Man's brother suspects him. But there's no proof."

"It's happened to other people too," she says gravely. "Creatures have been tortured. They found a dog with its bottom jaw ripped off, and a mutilated horse. There's somebody in this town who has violent tendencies, somebody with a weird head. There are some bizarros here."

I ask Wilma to describe her interaction with Cat Man's brother for me. "He came out here and was very upset," she says. "He couldn't get the police to do much. I had to help mellow him out a little. He came here with his car filled up with pistols and rifles. He came here ready for war."

I ask the room full of drinkers to raise their hands if they think Cat Man was murdered. Half of the six raise their hands.

"I think somebody was hunting a bobcat," says one guy in jest. More earnestly he adds, "Nobody would accept him because he mutilated his body. I think somebody killed him because he looked like a freak. And that was their opinion, not mine."

"No," replied one woman, "he was in this town way too long. He was established. People got used to him. If somebody was gonna murder him for that reason, they would have done it way long ago."

Jukebox

From my room at the Jim Butler Inn I can hear the music from the Tonopah Liquor Company, affectionately known as TLC. It's about sixty percent country music. The rest is hard rock, from classics like Guns N' Roses to '90s nu metal. Occasionally I hear what sounds to me like melodic screamo. I never hear top 40, hip hop, or R&B.

Inside the bar, which at this particular moment is playing Hank Williams Sr., I sit down next to two barflies, clearly already drunk though it's only half past three. One has a thick black beard and a serious expression while the other, older and smaller, sports grey stubble. The black-bearded one is talking to himself about the fate of the Confederate flag.

I've heard that the TLC's new owners, a young couple from Vegas, ban patrons who cause genuine trouble. These two are receiving friendly drink service, which emboldens me to ask them if they'd be up for an interview. The black-bearded one, Ray, blinks his glassy eyes and shrugs indifferently.

"What did you say earlier about the Confederate flag?" I ask to get the ball rolling.

"They shoulda never took it down," he says, staring straight ahead. "It should have stayed up." He slurs his words so I don't catch the first part of his next sentence, but it ends with something about "the pride of America."

"What does the Confederate flag mean to you?" I press on.

"It's a piece of history. It's like somebody taking your pictures and tearing them up and throwing them away. It's history, that's all."

I assume he's talking about the lowering of the Confederate flag in front of the South Carolina statehouse earlier in 2015. "Do you know why they took it down?" I ask.

"I have no clue," he readily admits. "I think it was a bad idea, though."

"Did you hear about the killing of nine people in Charleston?" He shakes his head. "Nine black people were killed by a young white guy who took lots of pictures of himself holding the Confederate flag."

"Well, that's a personal thing," Ray responds. "But the Confederate flag…" The pause is long, and I'm wondering if he'll finish. He swigs his beer and says finally, "is part of our history."

He's irritated with me. We both turn our eyes to the football game on the screen above the bar and I wonder if I should stop recording. But before I do, he says sneeringly, "You wanna talk to me about gay marriage?"

He has barely looked at me throughout our conversation, so I figure this is not an observation about my sexual orientation so much as a sarcastic reference to my prying on hot-button social issues.

"Sure," I say, calling his bluff. "What are your thoughts?"

He laughs and says, "That's fucked up!"

His friend, the skinny one who has been silently nursing a Budweiser up to this point, chimes in. "I don't care," he declares. His name is Walt, and he's significantly more sober than his friend. "I don't care what two consenting adults do behind closed doors. That's their business, not mine."

Ray puts his arm around Walt to illustrate the ridiculousness of this concept. "Look!" he says. "This is my husband-wife! Now you get to share my insurance and my social security!"

"Well, why not?" responds Walt.

"I mean, that's some stupid-ass shit," says Ray.

"That lifestyle would not be good for me, okay?" Walt says this more to me than to Ray, who is frowning. "But you know what? If they're happy, just let 'em be happy. All these people are living lies. Might as well be truthful about it. Nope, I'm not gay. Just so you know, I'm not. I'm not a homosexual." He repeats this several more times, then adds, "But it's none of my business."

Ray rises from his stool and drifts toward the jukebox, and Walt chats me up eagerly. He tells me that he, like Wilma, ended up here because his car broke down and he didn't have the money to fix it or move down the road. He's pushing sixty and has been in Tonopah for thirty years. "I like it here," he says. "Not a single stoplight. I like that. Are you a journalist? I like journalists." I hardly get a question in edgewise.

Johnny Cash comes on, and Ray returns slowly to his

seat. "Do you guys know Jeff?" I ask. Jeff is becoming a mascot of sorts. Everyone in town has an opinion about him, and the attitudes people hold toward Jeff – annoyance, amusement, sympathy, superiority – feel like clues.

"Why are you talking to us about Jeff?" asks Ray, mystified.

"A lot of people have mentioned him to me," I explain. "They say he's an interesting guy."

A stunned silence follows, and then the two burst out in laughter. "Did I hear that right?" says Walt. "That Jeff is an *interesting* guy?" The pair cackles at the absurdity of this suggestion for a while longer.

"No, he's not interesting," says Ray finally. He seems more clearheaded now, and less cagey. "He's a nice guy, and he wouldn't hurt ya, but he's clueless. Just a clueless guy."

"Every time you talk to him," says Walt, "he's gonna fall more in love with you. He falls in love with every woman he talks to. Other than that, hell, he's not that impressive. I don't know who told you otherwise."

Walt and Ray are unfazed by Jeff, probably because they occupy the same stratum of Tonopah society as him – a little dodgy but ultimately trustworthy enough to be welcome at the bar. I'm guessing that they, like Jeff, are Hank P.'s guys.

"What's your opinion of Hank P.?" I ask them.

"Ah, tread lightly!" says Walt. As I've been told already, a misplaced word about Hank can have serious ramifications.

"I love Hank," says Ray. "Very good friend of mine."

"Hank doesn't like me," says Walt. "I used to run the radio station here. And I was on the air one day when I said something about the local slumlord. I said I couldn't say his name, but his initials were Hank P." He laughs, but Ray doesn't.

I ask Ray to elaborate on his relationship with Hank P. He only says, "We have a big history."

"Hank doesn't like him either," says Walt.

"No, he loves me," protests Ray, and Walt snickers. Walt apparently has managed to stay out of Hank P.'s labyrinthine dealings, but I sense that Ray has been on both Hank's good side and his bad side. I ask if Hank is a decent guy, and Ray says only, "Heck yeah." Pushing Ray to expand upon anything has proved pointless, so I decide to move on.

"Hey, what do you guys look like?" I ask on a whim.

"How do you mean?" asks Walt warily.

"I mean I'm recording you, but when I listen back I won't be able to see you. So can you describe what you look like to me?"

The two sip their beers and think about my question. I'm surprised that it's Ray who pipes up first. "I'm scary," he says quietly. I detect a note of injury in his voice.

"Why do you think you look scary?" I ask. He's not wrong – he looks like a wayward biker stranded in Death Valley with only a bottle of Jim Beam to quench his thirst.

"Because I try," he says. I've struck a nerve.

"He just *is* scary," quips Walt, insensitive to Ray's contemplation. "Boy, imagine if he actually did try!" He cracks himself up, and Ray remains expressionless.

"What about you?" I ask Walt.

"I look like shit," he responds without missing a beat. I ask him why he thinks that. "Because I looked in the mirror today!" he shouts, and even the bartender laughs.

"We gotta play the jukebox," says Ray. He says he wants to hear Roger Miller, and asks me if I have any money. I fish out a couple quarters to contribute to the effort. He slinks toward the jukebox again, hands in his pockets.

Jesus, Little Wayne

The next day I spot Ray walking on a side street, headed toward the Super 7. I roll down my window as I drive past him and say hello. He seems pleased to see me and saunters up to my car window.

"You wanna meet some people?" he asks. I have no plans, so I say yes. He tells me to stay put while he buys some beer and he'll show me where his friends are hanging out.

After he emerges from the Super 7, I follow him in my car as he walks a few hundred feet up the hill. As I'm parking in front of the house he gestures to, I catch sight of the cross-streets and realize that this is the location of a notorious compound called Drunk Hill, where some of the old Club House regulars now drink all day. Several people have mentioned it to me, and their characterizations haven't been kind.

I consider turning back, but Ray is waving me over, and I've stepped inside before I've even made up my mind. The room is small and dark – a kitchen, with a fridge and a gas stove, but also a makeshift living room with seating and a television propped in the corner playing a football game. In this room are five white adults between the ages of thirty and sixty gathered around a small table covered in bottles and glasses.

The people turn to look at me, their faces creased with confusion. This is the most alien environment I've entered so far. But for some reason I trust Ray – this despite the fact that he appears to have sustained a mysterious facial injury since the day before. He's an alcoholic, that's evident, but he has a sullen equanimity.

I think back to our exchange about his perceived scariness, and I sense that by bringing me here he's trying to show me what his kind of scary looks like. Maybe he hopes that I won't be afraid. Or maybe he hopes that I will, just to confirm his suspicions. I take stock of my surroundings and decide there's no harm in staying for a bit, though I decline to sit.

"Mary Lou, I brought a girl," says Ray. He's speaking to a woman in maybe her early fifties who's sitting at the head of the table with a little dog in her lap. She sizes me up and nods her assent.

"She's a journalist lady," Ray adds.

"How cool!" says a second woman in her fifties, rail-thin and jittery. She shakes my hand and identifies herself as Rita.

"Do you own this place?" I ask the first woman, Mary Lou.

"Yeah," she answers, petting her dog in long, luxurious strokes. "But she lives here too," she nods toward Rita, "up there in the trailer with my brother."

"Is this where you guys hang out?" I ask to everyone in the room – the rest, besides Mary Lou and Rita, are all men. I learn that their names are Martin, Floyd and Little Wayne. Martin is a big guy in a Harley-Davidson shirt and a leather vest. Floyd's face is obscured by an unkempt beard and topped with a wide-brimmed cowboy hat. Little Wayne is young, probably no more than thirty, with a shaved head. He's dressed in an oversized white t-shirt and polyester work pants, a style reminiscent of West Coast lowrider culture, which seems out of place here. I learn later that he's from San Diego. His eyes are alert, clear blue, and trained on me in a way that I find immediately unnerving.

"It's my spot," says Mary Lou protectively, "and I decide who gets to come here. But you're welcome to stay. You want a beer?"

"No thanks," I say and take in the motley assemblage of glasses, cans, and bottles in active use. "Hey," I venture cautiously, "somebody told me about a place called Drunk Hill. Is this it?"

"Yep!" says Martin, and the room erupts in laughter, minus Mary Lou, who pets her dog with a frown on her face.

"No this is not Drunk Hill," she protests. "This is Lesterville. Because that's my mom's last name, Lester, and that's what this is – a ville."

"Once you come in here, you never leave," says Martin with a grin.

"Yes this *is* Drunk Hill," says Rita. "You're in the right spot." I sense people are warming to my presence. No one asks what I'm writing about, whom I'm writing for, or why I want to interview them.

"What do you guys do for fun?" I ask.

"Work, drink, gamble, fuck," says Floyd.

"Sex, drugs, and rock and roll," says Rita.

"Pink and green!" exclaims Martin.

"I like to play pool," says Little Wayne. I ask him where he plays. "I go to the TLC usually, but they told me I had to leave recently because somebody had a complaint about me. And I've been real nice."

"What do you guys drink?" I ask.

Rita holds out a small vessel shaped like an hourglass. The liquid in it is bright red. "This is a Jäger Bomb. Which is normally Jägermeister and Red Bull, but this one is vodka and Gatorade."

"I take a forty of Olde English," says Little Wayne, "and I mix it with Four Loko and put a little vodka in it."

"I only drink Tonopah water," says Martin. He holds up a bottle of Crown Czar Vodka and everyone laughs except Ray. I can feel him looking at me, trying to gauge my impression.

"What's your favorite bar in town?" I ask, though I think I know the answer.

"It used to be the Club House," confirms Mary Lou, "but they're dead and stinkin'."

I ask how everyone feels about the Club House being closed.

"I feel rotten!" says Rita.

"Sucks balls," says Little Wayne.

"Fuck, shit, fuck, hell!" yells Floyd.

"Let's go back," implores Martin.

"Fuck, hell!" repeats Floyd.

"I guess since the Club House closed, though," says Martin, "our favorite bar has to be Lesterville Bar and Patio." Everyone roars in agreement.

I ask how many people congregate here every day. "About this many," says Mary Lou. "Mainly me and my dog, and then it depends on my mood to let whoever I want in."

"She's the gatekeeper," says Martin. "She'll scare the hell out of anyone."

"After you leave she'll get in a bad mood and chase us off," says Rita. Mary Lou frowns with pride.

Little Wayne says something to me, but I don't hear correctly, so I ask him to repeat himself. He looks me dead in the eye and says, "I'd like to put you in a pipe and smoke you." It's unsettling, and the room is quiet, scanning me for a reaction. I decide to move on.

"Is Tonopah a nice place?" I ask.

"Yeah it is," answers Martin. "We're just on the wrong side of the tracks."

"We're the bad people," says Floyd.

"The bad kids," reiterates Rita, smirking.

"There are people who stay sober and are all uppity and do their thing," explains Floyd, "and we like to drink and have a good time." He raises his beer can.

"Ghetto style," says Martin, raising his drink as well.

"Are people scared of you guys?" I ask, pushing the envelope a bit, trying to see if I might be able to get to the heart of Ray's reason for bringing me here. Ray remains silent, watching intently.

"Well everyone's scared of Martin," says Mary Lou. Martin puffs out his chest. "We're all scared of each other, actually." I can't tell if she means this or not. Either way, she doesn't sound disturbed. She sounds obstinate, cocky, and protective of her brood.

"Nobody's scared of me," says Little Wayne. Later

someone tells me that Little Wayne moved here to start over after a history of substance abuse and trouble with the law, but he fell in with the same rough crowd again. "I'm not scary," he repeats, insistent. "People like me."

Then Little Wayne looks up into my eyes and says, "I have a question for you."

"What is it?" I ask. I don't enjoy his attention – it's too focused. He puts me on edge. I can tell that he, unlike the others, cares acutely that I'm here, and that the wheels in his head are spinning.

He speaks slowly and almost theatrically when he says, "What makes you think you're gonna get out of here alive?"

"Damn it," says Ray angrily. "What did you say that for?"

"Jesus, Little Wayne," says Mary Lou, shaking her head.

"That's my cue to leave," I say almost cheerfully, and am out the door before Little Wayne can say another word to me, though when I listen back to the recording I can hear him in the background saying, "Come on, I was kidding," as I'm exiting the house.

Ray walks out after me, and waves shyly as I get into my car. As I drive off I see him standing there in front of the house, hands in his pockets again, eyes on the ground.

Out of here alive

In the motel room, my heart rate returned to normal, I think about this exchange. Was I actually threatened? It's hard to interpret Little Wayne's words any other way. But more to the point, did he ever intend to do me harm? No, I decide, I don't think so. I suspect that, like Ray, he was floating a theory to see if it would be affirmed or dismissed. I had to leave Lesterville when I did, though, because I could've been wrong about the performative aspect of the threat. As a woman in particular, you don't stick around to confirm that kind of hunch.

A part of me wishes I could've stayed, though. "Bravo boys," I might have said. "You put on quite a show."

The people
I run with

I wander onto the middle-school campus as the sun is setting and follow voices to the gymnasium, where a volleyball game is happening. I gingerly ask someone at the door if it would be okay if I watched the game, and she smiles and lets me pass without further inquiry. Inside is Tonopah like I haven't seen it before: American as apple pie. The players are all braces and kneepads and swinging blonde ponytails. Young kids in the bleachers slurp from styrofoam soda cups the size of their heads, and parents talk idly among themselves or snap photos of the game.

Since I've been interviewing people as I meet them, I've mostly been talking to retail employees and bar patrons and the people they refer me to, letting chance guide me. I know this practice gives me a limited view of the town – it's easier to slide into a bar stool than into a chair at a family's dinner table. The people I see around me at the volleyball game are not exactly middle-class clean-cut – they sport camouflage hoodies and muddy boots at a rate unseen in your average suburb – but neither do they appear aged by poverty and intemperance like others I've met.

I think to myself that these must be the residents of the subdivision out by the courthouse, separate from the rest of town. The houses and apartments there are newer, built mostly in the 1980s. Unlike the ramshackle pastiche of the main part of town, in the subdivision you see basketball hoops affixed above garage doors at the end of smooth driveways and yard signs swearing allegiance to the Tonopah High School Muckers. It's a suburb like you'd find anywhere else in America, save for the fact that it abruptly falls away to reveal a stark, treeless expanse of unobstructed desert.

That's "the newer section," Mary K. explains to me from her desk at the town's H&R Block, which occupies the same building as the Tonopah Station casino. I met Mary at a POW MIA remembrance ceremony at the VFW hall. Mary organized the event.

"Anaconda or Sierra Vista, whatever you wanna call it," she goes on, talking about the subdivision. "It's a little ritzier, but it's not as ritzy as it used to be. It was for the new people in the early '80s. The subdivision was put in there because of the Anaconda mine, which used to be right behind the solar plant. They were mining molly. Mollybdenum, some kind of additive to process steel. When the steel industry went down, they closed that up."

Mary is in her late fifties with a warm and chatty affect, purple Coke-bottle glasses and a hairstyle reminiscent of another decade – short bangs poofed up high and long dirty-blonde tresses trailing down her back.

If Mary Lou is the den mother of Lesterville, presiding

over a daily gathering of drinkers and drifters, Mary K. is her inverse, the patron saint of all things bright and above-board in Tonopah. She seems to know everyone – several times during our interview she calls people I've mentioned to see how they're doing or corroborate a stated fact.

"You get folks who say, 'Oh, there's nothing to do in town,'" Mary tells me, "and it's like, what? If there's nothing to do in town, how come I never have any spare time?"

"Yeah, I've heard plenty of people say the town is dead," I admit.

"No, there's lots to do," she protests. "The only thing is, you can't sit at home and hope it drops in your lap. I meet women here who don't work, and I tell them to get out, get a part-time job, get involved in organizations. We've got the VFW and the Auxiliary, the Lion's Club, the Elks, the Rotary, 4-H. We have a group called For Our Kids that does Santa Claus and the Easter Bunny and a wonderful fireworks show." The list goes on.

"Tonopah is what you make it," she says in summation. "If you choose to see it as just a run-down town with nothing to do, that's what you'll get. If you can overlook certain things, then it's great."

Mounted on the wall next to her desk are several photographs of her holding a complicated-looking black machine gun and smiling before a backdrop of bare desert hills. Also on display is a kind of novelty rug, a photorealistic tapestry that depicts snapshots of her family – Mary, her husband, and her grown daughter, who is wearing a military uniform in most of the images.

Mary tells me she moved here from Illinois in the '80s, when her husband got a job at the test site. At first, she says, she was taken aback by the town's lack of amenities. "There's no Walmart, no Kmart, and that really impacts the way people live. In the '80s and '90s we used to drive three hours to Vegas every few weeks to get the things we needed. But we have the internet and can order from Amazon now. I've jumped on that bandwagon, don't mind spending a buck or two more so I don't have to go to Vegas quite as often. So yeah when I first got here it was a little rough, but I got involved in everything. I turned it around." She's brimming with enthusiasm for the town, a one-woman booster club. "Do I love it here? Oh yeah. You bet I do."

"And sure," she adds without prompting, "there's drugs and drinking here. If you don't see it, you've got your eyes closed. It all depends on the circle of people you're with. If you hang with that circle who happens to be involved with drugs, chances are you will be too. The people I run with, though, they're the outgoing types. They volunteer. You don't have to ask them twice."

I ask her if the town is a good place to raise a family, knowing full well that she'll answer in the affirmative. "Sure it is!" she exclaims. "The people are nice and the jobs are good. Working out at the Tonopah Test Range or for Round Mountain Gold, those are the jobs where you're making the most money. But besides that, you also have the school district, the department of transportation, the BLM, the forest service. Those may not always pay high salaries, but they have good benefits and retirement and they're stable."

I ask if there are any poor people in town. "You've got people who don't make a lot of money," she answers, "but the good jobs are available if you have the drive. You don't even need to have the education. You just have to not have a bad background – being into drugs, being arrested, those things will stop you from getting the good jobs."

"So yeah, we do have poor people in town," she continues, "but we also have people who aren't poor exactly, or they don't need to be. They just have learned how to use the government services instead of work. Those people are thinking they can get welfare, they can sign up for Medicaid, they can live in the apartments where the rent is based on income, they can get subsidized electric bills, they can get an Obama phone, and they don't have to do anything for it. The person who runs the Tonopah Apartments even used to advertise in the *Los Angeles Times* that he had apartments for cheap and there were a lot of social services you could get on here. So we started getting an influx of people from out of state who would come here because they knew they could get food stamps and government assistance."

She shakes her head disdainfully. "And if you're raised up in that kind of atmosphere, you're gonna go along with that, unless you're one of the smart ones who goes, hey no, I want to get a good job, I want to make an extra effort to become educated. I want to contribute to society."

"How do you feel about the Club House closing?" I ask, thinking her answer might further illuminate her perspective on the town's class hierarchy.

"The Club House was the place for undesirables," she says. "I went there on occasion and my friends used to say, 'You'd have a drink in a glass there?' And I'd say 'Oh yeah, the alcohol will kill the germs.'" She laughs warmly, then grows serious. "I did wonder, though, where a lot of those people ended up going. None of the bars now are the right atmosphere for those people, plus the Club House was really cheap. So I'm not sure. But I do see drunk guys sitting in that area, almost like they're mourning."

"Are you familiar with Lesterville?" I ask.

She winces with disapproval. "I don't go back in that area, you know."

Before we part ways she invites me down to the Bug Bar later that evening. She's making minestrone for bar patrons to share as they watch tonight's football game. "Everyone loves my Italian soup," she says. And I have no doubt that they do.

Desert rat

I meet Jenny and Caleb at the TLC. Mother and son, they share the same slight build, wide red mouth, high cheekbones and narrow eyes, the same sarcasm and bravado. Jenny tells me they're related to Judy Garland and I can sort of see it, especially in their eyebrows, which start high and form wide, graceful bows across their smooth foreheads. They're a handsome pair.

I'm captivated by their irreverent banter and no-holds-barred shit talking. They ask what I've seen of the town so far, and I tell them I've just been out to Crescent Dunes, the solar energy plant. Jenny sneers, "Oh, you mean Obama's golden phallus in the desert? What a money pit!" Caleb tells me they used to hunt and trap near the plant site – "Sorry if that offends you, Miss California."

Caleb comes to the TLC nearly every day. At only twenty-one, he drinks like a veteran of the trade. "I go through about a fifth of Jack a night," he says. I'm not sure if he's bragging or confessing. "Mark the bartender pours me double shots, and it takes me about six of those to get a buzz. So that's twelve shots at five dollars a pop just to feel something. Which is why I'm sitting on a seven-hundred -dollar tab at the bar right now." For her part, Jenny splits time between the TLC and the Bug Bar, a quieter joint with an older crowd.

I ask how they make their living. Caleb is a garbage-truck driver for the private contractor that handles all the waste in town. Jenny is on disability. In the winter, they set traps for wildcats, foxes and coyotes. "The money fur here is the bobcat fur," says Jenny. "I sell it on the garment market out of Fallon. I'm award-winning for foxes, cats and coyotes." She also develops her own essences, distilled scents like skunk spray that can be used as bait. The two enthusiastically describe a gambit they run selling kit foxes to taxidermists in Canada, where the species is protected.

I ask them if they'll be available for a longer inter-view the following day, Sunday. "Why the hell not?" says Jenny warmly. I suggest three o'clock, and Caleb cocks his head. The TLC isn't open on Sunday at three. I'm about to suggest a non-bar location when Jenny says, "Oh don't worry, the Bug Bar will be open." I arrange to meet them then and there.

I show up the next day to the bar atop the hill, a smoky Wild West-themed dive situated on the same plot as Humbug Flats, an apartment complex with an outsized number of motorcycles parked in the lot. Jenny is at the bar alone, sipping a vodka-cranberry and smoking Pall Malls, playing a poker game embedded in the bar countertop.

"Where's Caleb?" I ask, sliding onto the stool next to her.

She winces. "He got picked up for a DUI last night. He's in jail."

"Oh shit," I say. "I'm so sorry. Is now a bad time? I'm

sure you've got enough on your mind."

She puts out her cigarette and clinks the ice in her drink, beckoning the bartender. "I mean, I've got to collect money for bail, but that's really just waiting for people to call me back. So I can still talk, if you want." Maybe she's looking for a distraction, I figure. She motions me outside onto the patio, from which we can see the entire town and the desert beyond.

I'm planning to ask her about something else, but she starts talking about Caleb's situation straightaway. She says, "I'm trying to figure out how to come up with $855 before six o'clock in the morning, when Caleb has to be at work, or else he loses his job. I've got $700 coming tomorrow, but only after the banks open. Otherwise I got nothing."

I ask her what happened. She says Caleb ran into an old friend at the TLC, a guy he used to work with on a logging operation in Oregon. After last call, the two headed into the desert in the other guy's truck. Concerned that his friend was too drunk and driving recklessly, she says, Caleb offered to drive the two of them back into town.

"He got picked up by the most crooked cop in town. The officer has it out for him. He was just waiting for them to drive in. Busted him at the Super 7 when Caleb got out of the car to buy smokes."

Jenny's phone rings and she answers. I gesture to ask if it's okay to still record and she waves away my concern. It's a friend calling to say he can't help her with the bail money. "Sure, well if it was your left nut you were giving up, I know you'd do it," she says, "but your choppers, that's something different."

"So Caleb used to live in Oregon?" I ask when she hangs up.

"Yeah, I'm from there," she says. "Caleb was raised here, but he's got family in Oregon and he left a few years ago to go up there. He was a bit of a troublemaker here. He wanted to escape his reputation. He's got a beautiful heart, he just doesn't make the best choices."

"When did you move from Oregon?" I ask.

"When Caleb was just a kid, back in '06," she says. "I chose this place. I had just left my ex. I heard 'stupid fuckin' bitch' for the last time and drove off with Caleb in the clothes that I had skinned a deer in that day. And I had nothing. I had $38 in my bank account and 28 days to payday. I chose here because I'd checked it out before, and found that I loved it. I was born in Oregon up above a river. The townies called us river rats. So now I say I was born a river rat, I'll die a desert rat."

I ask her what she likes about Tonopah. "This is God's country," she answers. "This is the last bastion of free America. You don't have to answer to your neighbor for what you do. If you're not up to anything, you can open carry down the street. You can dig a hole in your own back-yard without a permit. And best of all, any place out of this three-square-mile area is the people's land."

The phone rings again, and it's Caleb calling from jail. The connection is bad. She tells him she's still working on scraping the money together. She says she's with "the journalist lady" – the second time I've been called this – but will track down a particular friend when she's done talking to me.

"Is he okay?" I ask.

"Sure," she says, unconvincingly.

I ask if the arrest is a red flag about Caleb's drinking

habits. "Oh yeah," she says. "But he's in a lot of pain. And nobody here knows why." I see that I was wrong about her searching for a distraction. She wants to dive deep.

"Why is Caleb in pain?" I ask, taking the bait.

She looks around the patio. There are two men in cowboy hats smoking and talking against the far railing, but otherwise we're alone. Still she leans in and speaks very quietly when she says, "He has leukemia."

"Oh," I say. "Fuck." This is unexpected.

"He's been misdiagnosed since he was thirteen years old," she continues. "They said he had osteoarthritis. He just found out last year. At the time he was stage four, but he's gone into remission. So he has a desire to live for the moment, you could say."

"Hence the heavy drinking," I offer.

"He's functioning, but his bones hurt," Jenny explains, "and there's nothing you can do for bone pain. That's why he drinks. And he has no medical insurance. He hasn't told hardly anybody, though."

"Did he come back to Tonopah after his diagnosis?" I ask.

"Yeah, but not to be taken care of," she says. "The opposite actually. I've started having real issues with my multiple sclerosis. I can't lift or move anything heavy. He came here to help me set up the house that I'm buying, so that when he wasn't here anymore I could be on my own."

She delivers this last line with a look of controlled anguish, and I'm not sure where I stand with her, what role I'm playing or purpose I'm serving. Maybe, I think, she needs somebody to talk to. And here I am, soliciting a conversation. She gets to be vulnerable under the pretense of doing me a favor.

"What's gonna happen to Caleb now?" I ask.

"Well, he'll lose his personal license, and his commercial license. If you lose your commercial driver's license you can't drive a garbage truck. In fact without a license, you can't hardly get any decent job around here." Even Crescent Dunes, the closest large operation, is a twenty-minute drive.

"It was difficult for me to trust him to come back," she says. "He burned a lot of bridges when he was here last time. He was a troubled teen, crashed vehicles, did drugs, stole some things. He's a little bit of a con artist." She lights another Pall Mall and looks out over the balcony railing at the quiet town and the long stretch of highway beyond, a faint gray trail cutting through a vast brown terrain. The sun is starting to set out past Crescent Dunes, and the headlights looks like a thin string of Christmas lights.

"Men are just little boys grown tall," she says. "Caleb has a very tender heart. But he's so young, he doesn't know how to deal with it."

"He's not happy," she continues, shaking her head. "His father was a happy drunk, but not Caleb. Caleb can get downright suicidal. This arrest is such a big setback for him. Not to mention he's sick. I don't know how this will affect him. I worry he's not gonna see a future for himself after this. I'm concerned about him, and I can't keep an eye on him. It won't be any use. He won't die in a hospital bed, I can tell you that. He'd rather drive out to the desert…" She doesn't finish this thought, and I don't blame her. We sit in silence for what seems like a long time.

"I didn't really need Caleb to come here," she says finally. "I made him think I needed him so he would come here. I can take care of him, while he pretends to take care of me. We can take care of each other. I don't know. I just gotta figure out how to get him out of jail before six o'clock in the morning. God help me."

"Are you religious?" I ask.

She closes her eyes, turns her face toward the sun, and holds her hands palms-up in a pose of divine reception. "This is my church," she says.

"The Bug Bar?" I ask dumbly.

"Not The Bug Bar!" I'm relieved at her laughter, and I laugh too. "We're looking at the sky, the mountains, the gorgeous desert," she says.

"People think it's barren, but it's not. There's a power there. I feel it when I'm out trapping and hunting. I feel nature, feel my family. Honey, you've gotta get off the pavement to see the true beauty."

A foot is nothing

The following night, Caleb agrees over text message to meet me at the Mexican restaurant, El Marques. It's quiet and well appointed, the kind of place families with modest disposable income go on weekly outings. The sign outside advertises a ten-foot television, and I wonder how this is possible, but when I walk in I realize they mean ten-inch. Caleb is sitting in a corner booth eating tortilla chips and sipping a soda.

"What happened?" I ask, though I know and he knows I do.

"That officer is a joke," he says. "He's on a power trip. He's trying to clear his name because he screwed up a while back and lost sergeant stripes. And he's got it out for me because I just got back into town, and I used to be a trouble-maker." He seems bitter but also a bit timid. I sense that his spirits are low.

The server comes by and I order a quesadilla, Caleb a bean-and-cheese burrito. I ask if he has a history with this cop.

"Oh yeah," he says, "he's arrested me several times. His boss used to be my neighbor though and would get me out of trouble. That pissed him off. Now that my neighbor is gone, I've got everybody up my ass." He slurps his soda. He's frowning and slouching in his chair, a wholly different creature from the cocky kid I met at the bar on the night of his DUI. "If it weren't for my neighbor," he says, "I'd probably be sitting in prison right now."

I ask him what for. "One DUI, one grand theft auto. But it was my own vehicle, so that was just a mistake. And then I did some stupid shit back about three years ago, stole a bunch of diesel fuel to go try to find somebody who'd been missing for four days. We ended up finding him but I got caught on camera."

"What were your teenage years like here?" I ask him.

"Believe it or not," he says, "I was a skater Nazi."

"Like a skinhead?" I ask. Having just conducted an interview with a one-time Aryan Nations member, I'm primed to interpret the word Nazi literally.

"No, that's just what my mom called us," he says, a little amused. "I was a skater punk. Skinny jeans and purple shoes and long hair. I was in a special ed class. I never fit in. And I found a group of people who were older who accepted me. I guess they figured, hey, this kid will do whatever we tell him to. He'll roll with it. That group got me into a lot of trouble."

"Are you still friends with them now?" I ask.

"A few of 'em, the ones that pulled their heads out of their asses like I did. But not the others. One of them's a tweaker, the other one we don't know where he's at. He got into drugs and no one knows what happened to him. And another one is sitting in prison for life because he smothered his child." I cringe. Caleb's circumstances are rough, but it occurs to me that he considers himself fortunate and well behaved compared to some of his cohort.

I ask him what kind of music he and his friends listened to. "Like metal, punk rock, I don't know. Avenged Sevenfold, Bullet for My Valentine, Godsmack."

Our food comes, and Caleb blows on his burrito to cool it. "We just skated everywhere," he says, "and if there was a rule to be broken we broke it. And my stepfather was abusive, used to beat me out in the hills when my mom wasn't looking, so that fueled the fire. I was in juvenile hall a lot, basically because I'd rather be in juvie than home."

I ask him what juvie was like, expecting his answer to be tinged with resentment. Instead he says, "Three meals a day, which was nice. It was kind of a co-ed deal. We had board games and got to watch movies. It was day care. When we were lucky we'd get to go on road crew, go out for pizza or something." He starts in on his burrito, and with his mouth half-full says, "I enjoyed the hell out of it, honestly."

"So it's not a sad or upsetting memory for you?"

"Not at all," he says. Then he explains that the juvenile hall in Hawthorne is very different from the juvenile prison in Elko, where he was also sent and where he ended up getting his high school diploma. "There was actual discipline there," he says, "military-style formations and all that, and real punishment. If you messed up you got put in a hot box. Solitary. It was a room eight feet by three feet. It had a chair during the day time, and they swapped that out for a bed at night." I imagine how these physical discomforts must have felt to someone with undiagnosed leukemia.

"Why did you have to go to juvenile prison?" I ask.

"Funny story," he says between bites. "You know me and my mom are trappers, so we have something called skunk essence."

He tells me that when he was a sophomore, his senior friends enlisted his help to prank the school. "I put it in a spray bottle for them and told them to go easy, don't spray anything that it can't be removed from. Well, they went hogwild. Opened all the lockers and sprayed everything in them. Sprayed the wrestling mats, the floor, the roofs. They sprayed everything that it don't come out of. It caused $289,000 worth of damage. So that's how come I went to juvenile prison."

He smiles a bit, but looks beleaguered. "I wasn't there when it happened," he adds. "I was at home asleep. But I already had so many strikes against me that they sent me off to Elko."

"Why did you have to go to juvie so many times?" I ask.

He says he can't really remember the order. He recalls that in sixth grade he stole a neighbor woman's wallet. "I was thinking there would be thirty bucks or something in there, but it was bill money, over four hundred dollars." He did a month up at Hawthorne, came out, failed a drug test and went straight back. "Another time I was leaving a party at the Belmont Apartments. I was out past my curfew since I was on probation, didn't have a driver's license, and I was drunk. I was driving off-road across the desert to get home. Some officers spotted me, so I flipped a bitch and tried to take off across the desert, but they caught me when I crossed Highway 6."

"You were driving off-road on purpose?" I ask.

"I always go off-road," he says, perking up. "I used to have to because I didn't have a license, but even now that I have one, hell, I like to take the trash truck off road. I don't like the pavement. I like the dirt better. In town I can only go twenty-five miles an hour and it drives me nuts. When I get out of town I'll do eighty or ninety across the desert. No roads, just screamin'."

I turn the conversation to the pending loss of his license. First he tells me that he'll be fine, he'll figure something out. He always does.

"Your mom seemed like she didn't think that's gonna be the case," I say. "She seems to think that if you lose your license, you're screwed."

"Well, you gotta drive everywhere to work. So there's that. But I know a guy that can maybe hook me up with a job as a mechanic out at Silver Peak, and I can post up in a trailer and just walk to work."

Silver Peak is a tiny mining community about an hour southwest of Tonopah, home to roughly a hundred people. I've never been but I've seen pictures of the lithium mine there, the only one in the United States. The tech entrepreneur Elon Musk is planning to use lithium from Silver Peak to power his Tesla cars. Other than that and a few news stories about a recent murder, there's scant information about Silver Peak online. People who work there often live in Tonopah, I'm told, because Silver Peak is not a very nice place to live.

"Does that sound appealing to you?" I ask.

"Well, I've got toys I can drive on dirt roads," he says. "If I wanted I could drive from Reno to Vegas on dirt roads. Four-wheelers, prerunners."

"Can you drive those things without a license?"

"No, but try and catch me out across the desert. You ain't gonna catch me." I recognize the bravado I encountered on the first night I met him.

"Well you seem pretty optimistic about it," I say. "Your mom made me think the opposite was true, that you were pretty scared." I wonder if I'm pushing too hard, but then decide that he can just keep up the swaggering routine if he doesn't like the line of questioning.

There's a long pause as he considers his options, and then he finally says, "Yeah. I feel like shit." The server comes by and clears table. Caleb continues, "I can put a hell of a face on. Inside, it's tearing me up. But, you know, I'm in public. I can keep from breaking down when I need to. It's like, people look at me and they say, he's the happiest person alive. You get me when it's just me, though, you know…" He trails off.

Then, sitting upright and perfectly still, he says, "I'm dying of leukemia."

He scans my face for my reaction. I'm not sure what he's hoping to see, or what he fears. I stumble a little bit. "I'm sorry," I say. It's ugly in its banality. He leans back against the booth cushion. A ranchera song plays softly over the speakers. He's disappointed in my reply.

"Hey, don't be," he says. "That's why I don't tell people, because I don't want people to be sorry for me. You know everybody's dealt a hand in life, and some people's hands are better than others. Some people have a royal flush, some people get a foot."

"What's a foot?" I ask.

"Not a hand," he says. "Get it? It's nothing. A foot is nothing."

We head to the front counter to settle our bills. Caleb grabs two Andes mints, and hands me one. Then he cocks his head and grins conspiratorially at me. "Hey," he says, "I think I've figured you out. You're a lesbian!" He laughs heartily for the first time since the night I met him, the night of his arrest. "Don't worry," he says, "I don't believe in it, but I'm not gonna give you a hard time."

Up until now I haven't mentioned being gay to anyone I've met in Tonopah; partly because it hadn't come up, and partly because I've assumed that journalistic objectivity would require me to go back into some kind of reflexive closet. Somehow, it hasn't occurred to me that in the act of looking I might be seen so clearly.

I don't wanna join your fucking biker gang anyway

I come down from the mountains around Lake Tahoe, headed toward Reno, and find a text message sent while I was out of range. It's a friend telling me I have to listen to some podcast, because a guy just called in saying he was writing a book about Tonopah. He's there right now, my friend assures me. I'm already en route when this conversation happens.

At first I'm seized by protectiveness, but I compel myself (not without difficulty) to be critical of that feeling. Tonopah is anything but mine, and truthfully I'm surprised it hasn't been written about more.

I find the writer, Christopher, on Twitter and ask if he'd like to meet up in town for a mutually beneficial recorded conversation. He sounds pleased by the prospect of my company. He's been staying at the Clown Motel for two weeks already on a self-designed writer's residency and hasn't spoken to many people (interviews are not part of his process). I settle into my usual motel, the Jim Butler, then head down to the Clown and knock on his door.

A big guy with a big beard and a friendly countenance, Christopher is a comic book writer by trade. "Scripts only," he explains. "I can't draw." We sit at the table in his motel room and talk about our motivations for coming here.

"I saw something about the Clown Motel on the internet," he says. "And I was like, a Clown Motel by itself is pretty cool, but then you learn about the graveyard, and the abandoned silver mines. I had to visit."

He drove out with a friend and got hooked. "Then we went back to Vegas and I dropped her off. I was gonna take some different route to get home, because these roads once the sun goes down are super terrifying. I thought I had punched in an alternate route, and I'm driving and suddenly I look up and I pass a sign that says 'Tonopah' and I was like fuck, I'm gonna have to stay at the Clown Motel again!"

Once he got back home to Portland, Christopher couldn't stop thinking about Tonopah. "For some reason I was like weirdly nostalgic," he says, "And there are these boring videos on YouTube of people just driving through towns—"

"I watched the same video!" I exclaim before he finishes. "When I got back to California, years ago. I did the exact same thing."

We laugh. "Yeah, I dunno," he says, "from there it just sort of turned into a weird idea I had in my head of, like, what if I went and spent a month in Tonopah at the Clown Motel. I kept mentioning it on Twitter as a dumb joke, but then I got some responses, and I thought, well, I wonder if that would work."

Frustrated with work and needing a break from Portland, he made a Kickstarter project on a whim. "And people were into it, or maybe they were just into the idea of sending someone they barely know to go live in a clown motel for a month and seeing how they mentally degenerate. Random people started giving me money. I'm still kind of baffled by the whole thing."

I ask him what his book will focus on. "I guess it'll largely be about me. I was thinking about it in terms of those books that pop up every now and then like *A Year of Living Biblically* or something like that. And I'll be writing about the town and how it has survived, and what it used to be. I had a buddy whose dad used to work at the Test Range and flew the stealth. Things like that. The idea of living in a place like this permanently is still, I mean, there's no hospital here. It's like, here's what you have and you don't get anything else."

"Yeah, and the really crazy thing about it too," I offer, "is there's a sort of strange human geography in this region. The federal government controls so much land around here that there aren't little towns scattered around like there are in other places. You can drive forever before you see something. You won't see trailers or houses out in the hills because you can't live out there. It's isolated in a unique way."

I ask him if he's learned anything surprising since settling in. "The good thing about this trip is getting to explore off Main Street. But, then again, things are a lot scarier once you get off Main Street. Something that hadn't occurred to me until about a week in was that, maybe you don't have to be afraid of clowns or ghosts, but people…"

"There's some trouble that you could get yourself into," I concur.

He nods. "Like last week, around midnight," he says, "I was kind of stuck on something so I was like, I'm just gonna go for a little walk up to Giggle Springs. I got the equivalent of a block or two up the road and there was no one around, cars coming like one every five minutes, and this creepy pickup truck rattles past me, and then its brake lights went on, and it pulled over to the shoulder, and they were just sitting there ahead of me, so I turned back. And it occurred to me that if I were to get grabbed off the side of the road, nobody would ever know what happened to me."

"Definitely," I agree. "It's hard to know the actual facts because there's a lot of hearsay in this town, and the police told me they can't discuss any criminal matters with me, but I know that this can be a violent place. There was a murder last year, and then a murder earlier this year. I mean, that's a lot. This is a pretty small town."

"Our boogeyman around the Clown is the Drunk Cowboy," he says.

"Oh, Jeff?" I say excitedly.

"Is that his name?"

"I think that's who you're talking about," I say. "I've never actually met him, though I've tried. He allegedly works at the Hock Shop and I keep going to interview him but he's never there. Everyone mentions him to me though."

"Yeah he first appeared last Sunday," says Christopher, "and it was raining and gloomy, and it was pretty raucous in the room next door. The Drunk Cowboy was there, and he got out of the room and was just wandering around saying 'Fuck you, fuck you.' It was like three in the afternoon, and he sounded drunker than anyone I've ever heard."

"I ran into him again on Thursday," he continues, "when

they called the sheriff on him. He was back here yelling things like, 'These motherfuckers are trying to starve me,' and 'I don't wanna join your fucking biker gang anyway.' I was sitting out by the graveyard when I saw him in his black cowboy hat. He walked right by the office and just flipped 'em off as he walked by. Then he went around to the back, and the sheriff showed up and went back there, but they never caught him. Jeff slipped away."

"I get the sense that people in town look upon him skeptically but also somewhat affectionately," I say. "Like, he seems to get away with a lot." I think back to a conversation I had with the owner of the TLC, who told me Jeff was his favorite customer, despite being a "wild card."

"Things can get a little dark here," Christopher reflects. "But I'm trying to focus on the good parts." I tell him I've been thinking the same. "The best thing for me," he says, "is that every day I look forward to going out by the cemetery and watching the sunset, because I'm not used to sunsets that look that good. And being out here I don't have any touchstones or rituals, so I'm establishing one of those."

"Are you feeling lonely?" I ask. I can't imagine staying here alone in my motel room, especially without interviewing people, for more than a few days.

"Yeah, yeah," he says. "It's nice to talk to somebody where you don't have to do the little 'who are you?' dance," he says.

"Who's the most interesting person you've met out here?" I ask.

"Well yesterday I met a guy working at the gas station at the edge of town who told me he had to go to home to six dogs, and he listed the dogs and was like 'and one of them's a wolf.' He was like 'Yeah he's tame, the Chihuahua even sleeps on top of him.' This is that kind of town."

"The bartender at the Bug Bar was great, too," he continues. "I asked her how she wound up here, and she said that forty years ago her mom was driving through and her car broke down."

"Oh yeah I met her," I say. "And actually her story is fairly common. I've talked to several other people who ended up here because their car broke down." The bartender at the Bug Bar had actually told me that there's a saying around here pertaining to this scenario: you cry when you get here, you cry when you leave.

"She's really nice," he says. "She also told me this was a good place for families. She was like, 'We have the same problems as any other place, a little meth here, a little booze there.'"

"Well I think there are different tracks you can be on in this town," I say. I tell him about the volleyball game, the Anaconda subdivision and Mary K. "I don't want my portrayal to be relentlessly grim," I tell him, "because that's disingenuous. But I also want to tell the truth, even when it is dark."

He agrees. "I have this audience that's expecting grim things," he says, "and I lean that way too. It's hard to put a positive spin on it. Or, I guess bleakness is a positive spin to a certain kind of person," he says. We're both worried about pandering to the coastal urban fantasy of bizarre backwater Nevada, cherry-picking the details that are most luridly fascinating without providing significant context.

"Hank P. told me he knows what I'm doing here," he says. I mention that Hank probably has his feelers out, because the Clown is gaining a cult following, which is great for business. "Yeah, and I was hoping to fly under the radar," he says, "because I didn't want them to think I was coming here as a joke, or to make fun of them or anything. That's not my intent. I just got fixated on the town and needed to come back."

"It's too bad you won't be here this weekend," he adds. "That's when we're doing the séance. My buddy used to be a magician who worked at The Magic Castle. He's pretty experienced at acting as a medium, all for entertainment of course. That was one of the stretch goals for the Kickstarter. We're gonna videotape it and show it to the donors. He guarantees results."

Still burning down there

I had envisioned Hank P. to be a kind of Godfather figure, charismatic and domineering. Instead he's soft-spoken and agreeable. I meet him in the lobby of the Clown Motel, where he's seated beneath an art poster that depicts painted clowns in outer space.

"I'm not sure if I'm a good interview subject," he begins. He's seventy-seven years old, but his skin is taut and tan, his hair thick, teeth white.

"Well, pretty much everyone mentions you," I say. "For instance, a lot of people who aren't from here originally, they say you helped them get on their feet."

He nods. "Some of them, sure."

"Why do you do that?"

"Well it's not just a matter of me just being a great guy, because I'm not," he says. "I need capable people, and when people fit the part and want to work, I put them to work. The labor force in Tonopah is pretty slim, and it's hard to find people that won't walk off a job and go get drunk.

Some of these people I give an extra helping hand, because I know everybody, so I can." And in return? "They're loyal to me."

I ask him how long he's lived here. "I was born here, and I've been here my whole life," he says. "My mother is a native Tonopahan, born here in 1920. My grandfathers both worked at the Mizpah mine."

"How has the culture of the town changed since you were a kid?" I ask.

"How hasn't it changed?" he responds. "We didn't have television until 1955. In fact, the first TV in town was installed by a guy named Pickles in an old mining tunnel out here. I had sprained my ankle, and I went up to his tunnel on crutches so I could watch the World Series."

"Why did Pickles put a TV in a tunnel?" I ask.

He shrugs. "That was the only place he could get reception."

I ask him how long he's run the Clown Motel. Twenty-one years, he tells me, clarifying that he took it over from the original owner. "Leroy was a good friend of my father's, and he owned this property. You see, Leroy's dad was one of the miners who were killed in the big mine fire and was buried in the graveyard over here. Leroy wanted to do something with the property. And meanwhile he had this collection of clowns that he picked up in Las Vegas."

"Did he like clowns?"

"I don't think he was ever a fan of clowns, no. But he had a complete bedroom full of clowns, so he decided to run with it. It's been here thirty years. I've tripled the collection of clowns since I came here. A lot of these clowns are from Europe."

"Do you get clown enthusiasts in here?" I ask.

"Oh yeah, all the time. And we get people who are very scared of clowns too. Sometimes people come in and they say, 'This is too many clowns. I'm getting anxiety.' For those people I cover up the clown portraits in the rooms, and we do the registration outside, so they don't have to stand in the lobby."

He continues, "Some people say they've seen ghost clowns in their room, but we haven't seen any. The Travel Channel came out here to find ghosts, and they won't tell me if they found any. I guess I'll have to wait for the episode to air. People see ghosts in the graveyard, and they hear noises coming from the graves. One guy had a deaf dog that used to perk up its ears and stare into the graveyard late at night. But I don't think there are any in the motel."

"So you believe in ghosts then?" I ask.

"Yes and no," he answers. "There's a connection that I have with the miners that died, because my grandfathers were miners and they worked underground with these people. Where all the miners died in the fire, up at the Mizpah mine, the shaft is still open. Because the air flows underground through the mines, it comes whistling out of there, making a crazy noise. And you can still smell all the smoke, like they're still burning down there."

He looks past me. "One day, fifteen years ago, I went up there and got close to it. I was looking for evidence of coyotes, which huddle next to the mineshaft in the winter because it gives off heat. And the earth gave way a little bit under my feet, so I stumbled backward. Something happened right then."

He straightens his posture and meets my eyes again. "It

was different. I didn't see no image or anything. It was just a different kind of thing that happened."

"Most people in town believe in ghosts, it seems to me," I say.

"I think you're right," he responds, adding, "and maybe they have reason to."

"What are the living people like here?"

"It's a good town," he says. "The people are good. I've always loved Tonopah. It's…" He tears up unexpectedly. At first I think maybe he's choking or about to sneeze, until he says, "I'm sorry, I get emotional because I'm thinking about my dad."

He clears his throat and runs his fingers across the desk surface as if to smooth it. "Tonopah was a great place for me to grow up in. We were poor, of course, and we didn't have a bathroom until I was in about eighth grade. But it's a great town. I've known so many people who come out for temporary work, and they finally decide they want to go back to their family or whatever, and I'll be damned if they don't come back within a few months. They return because they miss it."

I've heard less sentimental accounts of this same phenomenon. One person described Tonopah as a sort of landlocked Bermuda triangle.

"Is the town close-knit?" I ask.

"I think so," he says. "I have a big family, and my brothers and my sister and myself, we meet at my mother's every morning for coffee, and we solve all the town's problems."

"You mean you talk about local politics?"

"Everything from them closing the hospital, to so-and-so just died last night."

I ask him a question I've been dying to know the answer

to: did Hank himself shut down the Club House for the good of the town? He doesn't give me a straight answer. "The place was pretty divisive, you know. I tried to stay out of it, but there are drugs in Tonopah, and that was a big spot for drugs. And the people there drank and fought. The next person who takes it over, that's the first thing I'm gonna tell him: We need a nicer bar. I used to run bars myself, but those were different times. We had spaghetti dinners for everybody, and billiards tournaments and deer pools."

"What's a deer pool?"

"You bring your mule deer in, you pay an entry fee into a pool, and the person with the heaviest deer wins the prize money. We organized a lot of activities at my bars. I had lots of bars – the Pink Elephant Room, the Ace Club, the Pastime Club. And I had the bowling alley, called Silver Queen Lanes. Back when the town was a little more alive."

The phone rings and Hank answers. "Yes, she's here," he says. "I'm talking to her right now."

"Who was that?" I ask, bewildered, when he hangs up.

"Jeff," he answers.

"But I've never met Jeff!" I exclaim. Apparently he not only knows who I am, but is inquiring after my whereabouts. I'm nearly spooked, and then I remember that I started asking questions about him first.

"Jeff's a good cowboy," says Hank. "He's a loyal person to me, and he has a good upbringing. But he drinks."

I never do meet Jeff – this phone call is the closest I get. I yank the door handle of the Hock Shop nearly every time I pass, but he's never there.

"Do you foresee a big change in Tonopah's future?" I ask Hank.

"I think it looks really good," he says. "We have a new

gold discovery about twenty miles from here. And there's another low-yield gold mine right in town that's gonna open up soon. It takes three to five years to get a mine started. So that will be good for the town."

In ten or fifteen years, he says, the state's planning to construct a large interstate to run between Reno to Las Vegas. "I don't know how that will effect us, maybe good for tourism. I've been working here since the 1960s, and it's been a rollercoaster economy." He moves his hand up and down to emphasize fluctuation.

"But I see the future as good. Very bright. All we need is to get rid of Obama and for the price of gold to go up."

Grass is monotony

It's ten o'clock on a Friday, and the Bug Bar is closing early. I've come to find Jenny, hoping she'll fill me in on recent developments, but the only people in the bar are the bartender, Denise, and her sister, Monica. Denise is wiping down the counter, and Monica is smoking a long cigarette, singing along to Jethro Tull as she gambles on machine at the bar. The two decide they can stay open for a minute longer and chat.

"I have a dog named Katy," says Denise, "Katy Quaid."

"Why Quaid?" I ask.

"Because if I was ever gonna have a love child, it was gonna be Dennis's."

She opens the cash register to gather the receipts.

"I met Dennis Quaid once," she continues. "I was a limo driver in Vegas, so maybe 1991 or '92? Oh he was handsome." She makes a purring noise and then laughs from her belly.

"I first saw him in a movie with Kristy McNichol, when

I was in high school, *The Night the Lights Went Out in Georgia.* And I was hooked for life. I liked all the songs he sang, but I particularly liked 'Amanda.' So later, when I was in Vegas, I waited an hour an a half to meet him. There was a woman in front of me who sounded just like Minnie Mouse. I get up to the door and I'm gonna meet Dennis, and I'm the only person the bouncer isn't gonna let in. Dennis comes by and Minnie Mouse hands him a headshot and a resume, and you can just tell he's not interested. So I pick that bouncer up like a piece of paper and push him against the back wall and go up to Dennis myself. I grab Minnie Mouse and say, 'Off you go.' Dennis looks at me like, *thank you.* And I say, 'Dennis, how come you didn't play "Amanda"?' He looks me square in the eye and says, 'I wrote that song. I can't believe you remember it.' And we sat in a corner booth and talked all night."

Monica gets up and moves to the stool next to me. "It's true, you know. She really did meet Dennis Quaid."

"He was extremely nice," says Denise. "He could tell that I knew there was more to him."

"Are you guys from Tonopah?" I ask.

"Oh yeah," says Monica, "born and raised." Denise turns her attention back to the cash register, but Monica moves her ashtray between us and settles in to talk. "I did a stint in Arizona, a stint in Texas, but I'll never leave Nevada again."

"Why's that?"

"I didn't realize how beautiful it was before I left. I thought I had to be more around green and trees, but I'm a desert rat. And I have learned more about this area since coming back than I knew the whole time I was growing up here. I wouldn't have come back, but my ex-husband, he made me return."

"Was he from here too?"

"He was. We met in high school, broke up, went our separate ways. But I was back for a visit and he almost died. He got caught out in the snow, up near Manhattan. His car got stuck, just didn't make it over the mountain. Was left out all alone for three days. Hunger, frostbite. I saw him in the hospital and it brought us closer together, so we went ahead and got married. But then he died."

"How did he die?"

"Single car accident, out near Maggie Blues."

"What's Maggie Blues?"

"It's a little spot in the road, they just call it that. I don't know why. He lost control of the vehicle, rolled it. His alcohol level was way too high. I never knew how much he was drinking until after he died."

She considers this statement and changes her mind. "Well I guess I knew something. I thought love would fix it. But love doesn't fix alcoholism."

"Carry on Wayward Son" by Kansas comes on the jukebox, and Denise sings along as she records the day's earnings in a ledger.

"So he brought me out here, and then he died. But I stayed and I'm never leaving. Look at the mountains. Look at the colors and the shapes. I wish I was a geologist to understand the way the mountains were formed. I mowed grass in Texas on a tractor, Monday through Friday, and I don't want any more grass. I want dirt. I love the Indian paintbrushes. The lizards, the snakes, the horny toads. Why can't they put black sage after it rains into a scent, so I can smell it all the time?"

Billy Joel starts to play, but Denise shuts off the jukebox before the chorus. The lights behind the bar go out, and she jangles her keys to let us know it's time to leave.

"Grass is monotony," says Monica, grabbing her cigarettes and car keys off the counter. "It smells wet and claustrophobic. But sage has a smell that's wide open."

Veils and hazes

Driving south from Fallon on US-95, the towns get farther and farther apart. If the interstate project Hank mentioned is realized, this road will be a scenic byway for family vehicles. For now it's a workers' road, mainly big rigs.

None of these towns is identical to Tonopah, and none is identical to the others. Like islands in a loose archipelago, they share some features, but each is animated by unique logical principles.

"I could tell you how many steps make up the streets rising like stairways," Marco Polo says to Kublai Khan in Italo Calvino's *Invisible Cities*, "and the degree of the arcades' curves, and what kind of zinc scales cover the roofs; but I already know this would be the same as telling you nothing. The city does not consist of this, but of relationships between the measurements of its space and the events of its past." I've only studied the spatial measurements and past events of one town – Tonopah – but I suspect any of the others would yield as much.

Coming up on Schurz, on one trip to Tonopah, I observe a drab mist hovering over the town. Located on the Walker River Paiute Reservation, Shurz has a population of roughly 700, of whom almost eighty-five percent are Native American. If there is an active restaurant or general store in Shurz, I haven't seen it. I've seen only fireworks vendors, some in commercial buildings and others being operated out of crouched houses on debris-strewn lots.

Shurz is a sunken town, situated in a geological depression, and has actual trees. Most of them appear dead, though – mangled branches, the same mummified color as the earth. A homemade sign on the north side of town warns that meth is poison.

I feel the car drifting, and I steer to counter the wind. I soon find myself in the middle of a full-blown sandstorm. The wind threshes power lines, and tumbleweeds whip across the road. It's loud, like a vacuum cleaner. I stop the car and roll my window down to take a photograph, but sand flies in my face. Even after I've left Shurz behind – and with it, the "black blizzard" as it's called – I'm plucking granules from my scalp.

Beyond Shurz is Walker Lake, a gleaming natural basin that sustained human life in the region for 11,000 years. The Paiute call themselves Agai Dicutta, or trout-eaters – the precursors to counter-eaters. Their folklore often mentions a breed of giant sea serpents indigenous to the lake. Uncanny, since fifty-foot skeletons of ancient marine reptiles were located seventy miles away, in what is now the Berlin-Icthyosaur State Park. Today Walker Lake's shoreside boasts signs alerting visitors to tread lightly, lest they set off an unexploded military device.

South of the lake is Hawthorne, the closest town to Tonopah that rivals its size. Hawthorne is star-spangled – its facades sport red, white and blue decals, and patriotic bunting hangs from telephone poles. The Hawthorne Army Depot is the town's biggest job provider. To your right, as you leave town heading south, are rows of earthen mounds with doors installed in them and sage-spotted roofs, like Viking longhouses. This is the world's largest storage space for military-grade ammunition.

The highway leading out of town is segmented, each quarter-mile dedicated to veterans of a specific war. The last one is dedicated to veterans of the Global War on Terror. But the signs don't say whether they're referencing the preceding or forthcoming segment. The first time I notice these, I'm looking for some sort of marker to tell me that the last segment is over, but it never appears.

In Mina, a town of less than 200 people, I notice that the limousine that's usually parked outside of the Wild Cat Brothel is missing. The complex is unlovely – two double-wide trailers surrounded by faux Roman columns that hold up nothing. On a previous visit, a woman who had once been the madam of the Wild Cat had told me that the owner died and they were closing up shop. I had walked around the perimeter of the trailers once. The brothel wasn't taking customers, but Heart's "Magic Man" was drifting softly from one of the small windows.

Between Mina and Tonopah is seventy miles of desert. It's a difficult stretch to drive in the dark. With no lights or landmarks on either side, the road starts to feel detached from the Earth. It's easy to imagine losing control and careening into the jet-black oblivion. I prefer not to drive this stretch at night, but if I have to, I do it leaned forward, rigid, the car silent.

Light rain begins after Mina, intensifies, and then shades into sleet and hail. The sandstorm was just a preview, a bad omen. With the brights off, I can't see a thing. With them on, I feel like I'm zooming through a tunnel of stars.

I am afraid, and it occurs to me to look for a place to pull over, but I can't see anything besides thirty feet of pavement dotted with yellow paint. A truck passes me and I kill my brights so I won't blind the driver, which means that when it splashes water and ice onto my windshield everything is doubly dark. I start talking out loud, reminding myself to keep steady pressure on the gas, a firm grip on the wheel. I try to focus on the road but my eyes are drawn slowly and continuously upward into the conical vortex of falling ice. I shake my head violently every minute or so, trying to jostle myself to attention.

When Tonopah's lights appear, I rejoice. I feel I'm alighting on Paris – the streetlamps and the Clown Motel's flashing marquee bulbs seem astonishingly cosmopolitan. Tonopah is a shaggy little town, but coming in from the desert, it looms large, an electric miracle in the annihilating dark.

Tonopahans have a genius trick up their sleeve, a technique that helps them thrive in isolation. They know that exposure to the desert can alter perception like a narcotic. If they find they're getting too used to civilization, and the town is looking a bit run-down, they go out and terrify themselves in the badlands. They drive their motorbikes and four-wheelers into the ground, out somewhere near Silver Peak or up toward Mina, and then load them into the backs of their pickups, destroyed, to be displayed out in the yard.

Sometimes they crack their skulls doing this. But the point is to crack the mind. Unobstructed sightlines, infinite clear air, throbbing silence, sand, wind, acid light or pitch black, veils and hazes, speed and birds and blood and thirst. If you go deep enough, the Great Basin desert can convince you that only it exists.

Upon return, Tonopah has all the amenities of paradise.

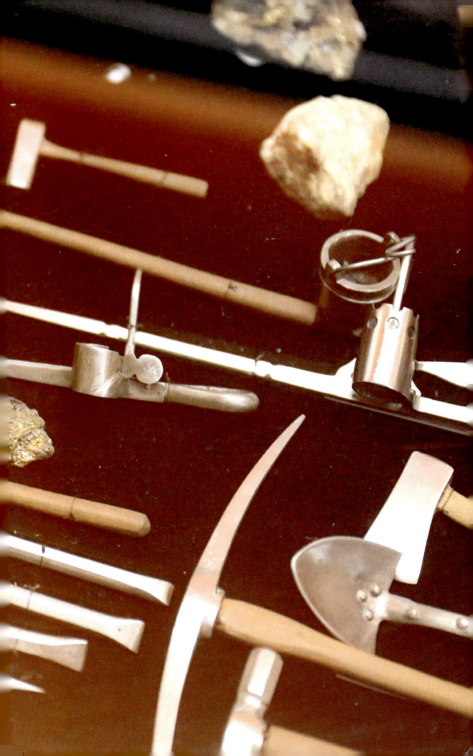

ACKNOWLEDGMENTS

Most importantly we want to thank the people of Tonopah, without whom this book would have neither shape nor purpose. Most of their names have been changed to protect their privacy. We'd also like to thank Justin Carder, Stephen Steinbrink, Erica Schapiro-Sakashita, Nina Aron, Helen Stuhr-Rommereim, Jimmy and Jennifer Day, David and Yolanda Klein, Ben Klein, Dakota Day, Carson Day, Marty Cortinas, Scott Beauchamp and Michael Schapira for their collaboration and encouragement.

E.M. Wolfman
410 13th St.
Oakland, CA
94612

1st Edition
Printed in Michigan

WOLFMANHOMEREPAIR.COM